DON'T LET YOUR PAST HOLD YOU BACK

THE REDEMPTION OF A GANGSTA

M. LAMONTT BOWENS

outskirts
press

Outskirts Press, Inc.
http://www.outskirtspress.com

Paperback ISBN: 978-1-4787-9434-9
Hardback ISBN: 978-1-4787-9634-3

Outskirts Press and the "OP" logo are trademarks belonging to Outskirts Press, Inc.

PRINTED IN THE UNITED STATES OF AMERICA

Gloria Ann Bowens

"Let not your heart be troubled; you believe in God, believe also in Me." (John 14:1-1 *NIV*).

Table of Contents

Introduction

Don't let the title of this book mislead you. As it suggests, I'm a re-formed gangsta, and the days of aspiring to be a black Al Capone or an inner city emulation of Al Pacino's motion picture character Scarface is in the distant past. I do warn the reader, however, this is not a story about some exceptional black kid from the ghetto who makes good. In fact if you're looking to read a feel-good story about some inner city black kid who resisted the negative temptations of his environment and somehow beat the odds, you might be in for a disappointment.

Although it's an accurate account of my life with a lot of ugliness when I was at my worst, I try to convey a message of hope. I was able to turn my life around and believe there is no reason someone else can't do the same. If I can do it, so can you.

I finally decided to write this book after being encouraged by family, friends, and colleagues to tell my story. I had initially resisted telling my story out of fear of embarrassment and shame. In fact, there is no question that I could lose some acquaintances and career opportunities from writing this book. I could have sugarcoated my story by trying to come across as some success story and portray myself as something I'm not, but I couldn't sell myself short or sell you short as the reader. I tell my story in the rawest no-holds-barred way, the only way I could write a book about my life.

I eventually beat the odds, but it would take many years of overcoming terrible decisions that I made. Some of the things I've done I'm just now having the courage to discuss openly outside of my close circle of family and friends. This book details in depth, and at times unpleasantly, how I became a hardcore gang member, a high stakes drug dealer, a federal prisoner, and then ultimately turned it all around and became a lawyer. I own my past, and I'll continue to move forward with dignity. Don't Let Your Past Hold You Back.

I Wasn't Born a G

POW! I HAD heard that sound literally a hundred or more times a week and knew exactly what it was. Hearing gunshots was not out of the ordinary for me. In fact, if I didn't hear gunshots I probably couldn't sleep at night out of concern something was unusual. But on this particular night when I came outside, I was devastated looking at my nigga Lil Crazy lying there on the concrete motionless with his brains blown out. I was not prepared for what I saw. I'll never forget it.

I had already lost a number of friends to violence but this one was too close to home. Lil Crazy was a close friend and had just left my spot not even five minutes earlier. We were just laughing and talking shit to each other while drinking. Now my dude is gone. Here he is, lying next to my car in a pool of blood.

I thought about giving up gangbanging that night Lil Crazy got shot. And I actually put away my guns until the following morning. But I couldn't let that gang shit go. I had ambition to become a rich drug dealer, too. The only dream I had at the time was to die young and be remembered as a martyr for my gang, or in the alternative, become a rich drug dealer who ultimately would spend the rest of his life in prison. Looking back that was a sad and crazy way of thinking. At the time, it didn't seem sad or crazy at all to those in my inner circle. It was a way of life—and death. Less than a year after losing Lil Crazy to the streets I would be standing in front of U.S. District Court Judge Edward Rafeedie, waiting to be sentenced to the federal penitentiary at the age of nineteen.

Contrary to common belief, not all people in the inner city join gangs by choice. It certainly wasn't that way for me, and neither was it for most people I grew up with. Most gang members do not wake up one morning saying, "Today I'm going to be in a gang." From my experience, it almost never happens that way.

Yeah, I know with the internet and social media being so prevalent now that almost anyone can wake up one morning and upload a gangsta rap song to YouTube or post some menacing things on Instagram or Twitter and suddenly he or she is a gangster. I'm not talking about internet gangsters, I'm talking about the real thugs, real street gangsters who actually grew up around gangs and actually participated in its activities to the fullest.

For most gang members, gangbanging and committing crime are a way of life and typically starts at a very young age. Gang members* are usually exposed to gang life and crime sometime in elementary school and maybe even earlier. It's not unusual for a gang member to have a father, older brother, cousin, or some other person in the neighborhood he or she looks up to who happens to be in a gang.

Although I do not make any excuses for gang violence or crime, I understand why some people join gangs and become violent and commit crime. My introduction to gang life wasn't a well-thought-out choice; it was more of an automatic rite of passage. And this rite of passage is particularly true for black and brown males living in the notorious inner-city streets of Southern California.

The most vivid and memorable events growing up began when I was around seven years old in the predominately black and Latino area of Southeast San Diego. It was around 1977. I lived with my parents and my four older siblings. We lived in a four bedroom two bathroom single-story house in one of the nicer-looking areas of Southeast San Diego—at least that was my perception at the time. The area I lived in was called Skyline. Back then Skyline had mostly single family homes, and many of them were well kept and had manicured yards. It was definitely a working- to middle-class black neighborhood similar to what Compton, California, was in the 1970s and early 1980s.

Back then there was only one apartment complex in the whole neighborhood, and it was called the Meadowbrook Apartments, a large multi-apartment complex similar to what may be considered a nicer-looking housing project. Although the Meadowbrook Apartments looked nice on the outside, I do remember it having a notorious reputation even back in the 1970s.

Prior to turning seven years old, I don't recall having any worries that would be different from any other kid who was growing up in a two-parent home and in a working-class community. I was the youngest child living in a nice house in a decent neighborhood, and besides trying to make it through the day without getting a whooping from my mother for doing something I wasn't supposed to do, my life was relatively normal. I also had a house full of older siblings who looked out for me. Life wasn't perfect, but I can honestly say I don't recall any instances that had any lasting negative effect on me during this time. In fact when I look back prior to turning eight, I couldn't have asked for a more normal childhood.

My mother was a homemaker and my father worked on a military base as an aircraft painter. I was only seven years old and may have been oblivious to my family's real socioeconomic status. I had always felt safe and comfortable, and I never had to worry about whether I was going to have enough food to eat or a place to sleep. I can also recall having gifts under the Christmas tree every year and occasionally my whole family taking overnight fishing trips where we would all sleep in my father's camper that was attached to his truck. I may not have been living like the Huxtables from *The Cosby Show*,* but I definitely was not poor or preoccupied with thoughts of gangs or crime.

Life was good for me at home, however I was aware of the existence of gangs and criminal activity around the neighborhood. I always felt like I was shielded from the inner-city realities that existed around me and I never had to give it much thought. However, little did I realize that my seven-year-old ideal childhood would end within a matter of months.

Initially nothing seemed out of the ordinary. My father occasionally came home late from work, and sometimes it would already be dark, so it was not unusual for my siblings and I to already be getting ready for school the next day by the time my father got home from work. My evenings as a seven-year-old kid were usually uneventful unless my siblings were arguing or fighting, which was a common occurrence in our house, or someone got in trouble and my mother was yelling at him or her.

On one particular evening, however, it was far from uneventful. As soon as my father walked in the front door, he and my mother began arguing. My parents had argued on a number of occasions, so I assumed it was no big deal and it would die down after a few minutes, but this time it was different. The argument lasted longer and was more intense than usual. I was in the vicinity of the kitchen where my parents were arguing, probably being nosy and trying to eavesdrop. I had never seen my parents hit each other, but I was definitely afraid that it was going to get physical because of my mother's anger. My mother was shouting at the top of her lungs right in my father's face. Within minutes my brothers and sisters were in the kitchen or standing nearby listening to my parents argue. This scene took place about forty years ago, but I still vividly remember my father slapping my mother and then watching my mother grab a kitchen knife and chase my father through the house and then out the front door onto the street. With my mother being in hot pursuit with a large kitchen knife behind my father, I watched in horror as my father attempted to open his car door with his keys so he could jump in and drive off. He didn't have enough time to open his car with my mother only several feet away from him, so he ran down the street. Fortunately for my dad he was able to run a lot faster than my mother.

I would learn a few days later, probably from eavesdropping on my older siblings, that my parents were fighting because my father was having an extramarital affair. My mother had become aware of my father's cheating and waited to confront him once he got home from work.

A few weeks after my parents' big fight, my father officially moved into his own place and then eventually moved in with the woman with whom he was cheating on my mother. He and my mother would eventually divorce and he married the other woman.

I was seven years old and the world I had been accustomed to changed almost overnight. I was still living in the same house I grew up in and I was going to the same school and had the same friends. I was still living with my mother and my sisters and brothers, and I would visit my father on the weekends.

Although things were still relatively normal—for me anyway—within a few months I began to notice things going downhill for my family. The middle-class "ideal family" reality no longer existed. There was no longer the strong family unit, and it was beginning to show in all kinds of ways and I started to become more aware of my ghetto reality. My childhood was now becoming dire and desolate.

DON'T LET YOUR PAST HOLD YOU BACK

My brothers, who were in their early teens at the time, began running the streets more. My sister Rhonda, who was the oldest in the house, started having more boyfriends. My mother became more introverted, was suffering from depression, and self-medicated with alcohol and marijuana. With a father figure absent, my mother was trying to raise five kids in the inner city of Southeast San Diego, and my innocence as a happy-go-lucky child with no major worries in the world would soon be taken away.

CHAPTER **2**

The Streets Are Calling

AFTER THE DIVORCE of my parents it didn't take long for me to start experiencing crime or at least recognizing it when it was in front of me. One instance that still resonates with me happened while I was sitting in my house on the floor in our den watching cartoons. Suddenly my brothers and one of their friends walked in with a huge duffel bag. The friend immediately poured all of the contents of the duffel bag on the den floor not too far from where I was sitting. There must have been several thousand coins poured on the floor. I wasn't sure how much money it was, but there were hundreds of quarters, dimes, nickels, and pennies— maybe even thousands. Even though I was only seven years old and somewhat naïve to my inner-city surroundings, I quickly realized what was happening.

Although I knew the money had been gained by some unlawful act, after listening to my brothers and their friend talk while counting the money, I would learn that the friend had just stolen the money from an armored truck and made a quick getaway to our house. Shortly after the armored car theft, I would have several more experiences that would further introduce me to a world where criminality would become my reality rather than something to be indignant over.

Although those early experiences of criminal activity were rare occurrences for me, I'm almost certain there were more like them that I was unaware of. Gradually I would become keenly aware of what was going on around the neighborhood and in my house in particular. Hearing about house burglaries, robberies, and violence throughout the neighborhood started to become more intriguing for me. Once naïve to my inner-city realities, I was starting to get prepared for the inevitable life that awaited me.

It had almost been a year since my parents divorced. I was too young to understand the particulars. My brothers eventually moved in with my father and his new wife, which in many ways turned out to be a blessing for my brothers because they were able to escape most of the realities of the hood that I would eventually experience. My sisters went to live with my grandparents in Bakersfield, and my mother and I stayed in the house in San Diego. Within a few months, however, my mother and I joined my sisters at my grandparents' place in Bakersfield.

I had visited Bakersfield a number of times so I was already familiar with the city. What I remember most about Bakersfield during this time was it was scorching hot. My grandparents lived out in the country where all of their neighbors had mini farms with all kinds of animals, and most of their neighbors were white, with the exception of maybe one other black family. After living with my grandparents out in the boonies for several months, my mother and I eventually moved into our own place in the inner-city part of Bakersfield on 8th and N Streets on the Westside.

Bakersfield may have been considered a small country town at the time, and probably still is, but it already had started to experience a serious gang problem. My sisters stayed with my grandparents and were enrolled in school near my grandparents' house but would visit my mother and me almost every weekend. They didn't visit us every weekend because they missed us; it was because we lived in the city where most of the other black people lived. It was just more exciting than being in the middle of nowhere about thirty minutes outside of the city living with two old people.

Whenever my sisters visited on the weekends, all of the boys in the neighborhood would somehow make their way over to our house or on the block. My sisters were the new pretty girls in the neighborhood and I'm sure all the guys couldn't wait for the weekend to see the Bowens girls and vice versa. In fact, my sisters never passed up an opportunity to come over, and within a year my sister Sonya moved in with my mother and me, and then my sister Rhonda followed about a year later.

I went from eating three hearty meals every day with plenty of leftovers and then within a couple of years barely having enough food to eat. My mother had become dependent on government assistance for all of our basic living necessities. It was only on the first and fifteenth of the month and a day or two that we had plenty of food to eat. During this time I'm not sure if my father was giving my mother any money for living expenses.

Even with the public assistance we were receiving each month, it seemed like we rarely had enough money for food to make it through the month. I had adequate clothing but never anything particularly nice or with name brands. Not having name-brand clothing wouldn't bother me much until I was older, but by the time I went to the seventh grade, the way I dressed would have a dramatic impact on my confidence.

My mother had always been a homemaker while she was married, so I think she never gained any employable skills outside of the home. Couple this with the fact she was devastated about the breakup of her marriage and family, I don't think my mother ever recovered emotionally, and it prevented her from ever having a serious desire to go out into the world and seek employment in earnest.

DON'T LET YOUR PAST HOLD YOU BACK

While I lived in Bakersfield, my sister Sonya and I would go to San Diego to visit my father and brothers during a couple of summers. My brothers also came up to stay with us in Bakersfield one summer, but other than the two summers and one Christmas, I didn't have a lot of contact with my father after I left San Diego. My father moved to Florida when I was around ten, and I wouldn't see him again until I was sixteen years old.

Bakersfield is only a couple of hours drive from Los Angeles, and its inner city had no shortage of gangs and crime when I got there in the late 1970s. In fact it was Bakersfield, not San Diego, where I was first indoctrinated with gang culture. I was around nine or ten years old and my sisters started dating guys from the Stroller Boy Crips which was a well-known gang in Bakersfield. I had no father figure or any positive male role models around, so these guys became the older males I started looking up to. I was at an impressionable age and I was also intrigued by how my sisters' boyfriends and their friends acted. They were tough or at least played the role as tough guys very convincingly. We lived in a rough neighborhood, so being tough was definitely a good attribute to have.

After I reached the age of eleven, I wanted to be more like the OGs (original gangstas) in the neighborhood. I was in what you would call a gangsta afterschool program. When I was around my sister's boyfriends, most of my friends my age and I were eager participants in the indoctrination of gang culture. My best friend, James, who I called my cousin, lived next door. Although James was only a year older than me, he was already well acquainted with the streets and knew the street life more than I did. His mother was a single parent like my mother, but James' mother had given birth to him when she was a teenager. Unlike me, James never had a father in the house, and he was being raised by a teenage mother and the streets. In fact James was actually growing up along with his mother, and she gave him a lot of leeway that my mother would never give me. James was already allowed to smoke weed and had been getting high since he was around eight or nine years old. Along with my older sisters and their boyfriends, hanging around James definitely got me up to speed with the street life.

James and I were learning the gang culture at lightning speed by watching the older guys. We would stand in front of our apartment complex and watch the OGs shoot dice, drink Olde English 800 malt liquor, smoke weed or PCP aka sherm, speak gang lingo, and listen to gang war stories. I was only eleven years old and not in a gang yet and didn't have any war stories of my own, but it was mesmerizing to hear the older cats talk about the fights and shootouts they had been in.

Around this time I was also starting to get exposed to various weapons, including guns and knives. James and I started carrying concealed switchblades, which was the popular street knife at the time. We had absolutely no enemies but carrying weapons was what you did, even if it was just a knife. If nothing else it made us feel cool.

One of my first experiences with a gang confrontation involving guns happened when I was eleven years old while standing right in front of the entrance to my apartment. Although my sisters dated mostly Crips* from the Eastside, we lived in a predominately Blood* neighborhood on the Westside and it was the Westside Warlord Bloods gang territory.

During this time in Bakersfield the Westside Warlords was the only Blood gang. I recall them being much smaller in numbers than the Crips on the Eastside. On the Eastside you had two Crip gangs, the Mid City Crips and the Stroller Boys Crips who were allies at the time. Since the Warlords were a relatively small gang in comparison to the Crips and they had no allies of their own, a lot of the Crips took advantage of this and hung out on the Westside.

DON'T LET YOUR PAST HOLD YOU BACK

One night while I was hanging out with my sisters and their Crip boy-friends in front of our apartment, some Bloods we knew from around the neighborhood walked up to us. There was a brief conversation between my sisters' boyfriends and the Bloods. I remember the scene like it happened today. Out of nowhere one of my sister's boyfriends pulled out a handgun, and my other sister's boyfriend pulled out a sawed-off shotgun. The strange thing was I wasn't afraid and didn't try to hurry inside our apartment. I just stood and watched, anticipating what was going to happen next.

My sisters' boyfriends pointed their guns in the air and pretended to shoot. In hindsight I realize now that they were trying to intimidate or scare the Bloods, but the strangest thing happened instead. Within a couple of minutes of this interaction between some Crips and some Bloods where guns were involved, all of a sudden the guns were put away and my sisters, their boyfriends, and the Bloods started smoking weed together. All I remember is everyone smoking weed, Crips and Bloods, my sisters, all in harmony. Funny what a little weed can do to calm nerves and make peace, and the peace pipe was definitely on display that night. I don't know what actually deescalated the situation, however; I doubt weed alone did it, and even though the night ended peacefully, the tension in the air remained thick.

Although there was no shooting or fight that night, in the following months my sisters became targets for some of the girls in the neigh-borhood who associated with the Bloods. My sister Rhonda ended up getting jumped by these girls on several occasions, and the Warlords even threatened to shoot up our apartment.

Believe it or not, even though I had already experienced a lot of ille-gality by the age of eleven, I was not involved in any criminal activity. Most of the kids my age were stealing candy from the store or stealing bicycles, but nothing too serious. Although I hadn't started commit-ting crime yet, one thing I did pick up was drinking alcohol. I started drinking alcohol regularly around this time. Inner-city life was tough, and being poor and on welfare made it even tougher for me, so I self-medicated with alcohol. I realize now that it gave me a temporary escape from my reality, and I needed it to cope. Furthermore, I was always a short, skinny kid, so it even gave me some much-needed liquid courage. There was never a shortage of people willing to try you in the ghetto, and fist fighting was an everyday way of life. Although drinking seemed to help at the time, in hindsight I know it did more harm than good.

I wasn't involved in sports growing up and I wasn't very artistic either. I don't recall having any positive role models around, so I spent most of my time hanging out and getting drunk. Unlike drinking alcohol, however, for me smoking weed would not come until later. Initially I was afraid to smoke weed, even though everyone around me smoked it. My sisters, their boyfriends, James, and even some other kids my age I hung around with were already weed smokers, so it was just a matter of time before I tried it. At first, because I was still nervous about the effects of smoking weed, I pretended to inhale; however, that behavior lasted only a short time, as people called me out for wasting their weed.

The first time I actually inhaled while smoking weed was a hallucinating experience. My mother was gone one night and it was just my sisters, their boyfriends, and me in our apartment. My sisters and their boyfriends were all in the living room smoking weed, and I decided to take a hit and inhale this time. After several hits of the joint, all of a sudden I remembered that the next day was a school day. I had never been excited about going to school before, but the THC in the weed hit me, and I began running around my bedroom jumping up and down on the bed in my underwear yelling, "It's school tomorrow" to the amusement of my sisters and their boyfriends. Needless to say, I've never been a big fan of smoking weed.

DON'T LET YOUR PAST HOLD YOU BACK

Even though I didn't really enjoy the kind of high I got from smoking marijuana, the peer pressure to smoke weed was intense since almost everyone in my world either smoked it or sold it or both. I wasn't much of a leader back then and was susceptible to pressure. I knew if I wanted to be considered one of the young cool dudes in the neighborhood and be perceived as older than I was, I had to partake in marijuana smoking. It was just a way of life for most of the people around me, or at least that's the impression I had.

By the time I was eleven, drinking alcohol and smoking weed were an almost daily ritual for me. Some people may think it's unfathomable that someone at eleven would get high daily, but where I'm from and how I was raised, it was not only normal it was almost expected. Of course not everyone my age in my neighborhood smoked weed or got drunk, and there were a lot of good kids in my neighborhood with similar backgrounds to mine. However, what bothers me is when I hear people, usually people who have never lived in the ghetto or never had to experience it in any defining way, say "Oh, this person or that person made it out of the ghetto without ever getting into any trouble or doing drugs, so how come you couldn't, or why can't you?" When I hear this, my response is always the same: "Well, good for them."

Everyone isn't the same and not everyone's experience in the inner city or ghetto is the same. Some people have both parents in the house; yes, even in the ghetto. Some people have a single parent who is mentally and emotionally stronger than others in keeping a child on the right path. And people, wherever they live, have different talents, gifts, and opportunities. Yes, there were a lot of kids my age in my neighborhood that weren't smoking weed, who weren't drinking alcohol, and who did not join a gang, but the majority of them did.

It's misleading when people point to one person out of a thousand as an example of what you should have become. That one person should be looked at as an example and as someone to emulate or aspire to be like, but it shouldn't be used as a definite measuring point while overlooking or whitewashing all the things that are preventing the other 999 people from succeeding. There's only one Michael Jordan. There's only one Oprah. And yes, I could have been the next world renowned brain surgeon, Doctor Ben Carson, but the odds were astronomically against me.

I think one of the most devastating effects for me growing up in the hood was watching the older guys go in and out of juvenile hall, jail, and prison. I thought such things were an inevitable rite of passage. By the time I was eleven I started to believe I had to prepare myself for incarceration. In a strange and twisted way that could be understood only by someone who grew up in the inner city and who was actually a part of the street life, I somewhat looked forward to the day I could brag about having been locked up. To us in the hood, it was a street-life graduation, a badge of honor, to say you did time.

We were all young thugs in the making, and getting locked up was just another part of growing up. Having those ghetto dreams of one day getting the proper street cred from doing time in the California Youth Authority or prison was something we thought about often. It's sad as I reflect on it now, but the guys who got locked up were like celebrities in the neighborhood when they came home. At eleven years old, although I was still far from a tough guy or gangster, I was adjusting to my environment, and each day I mimicked those I related to and idolized more and more.

When I was halfway through my sixth-grade year in elementary school, my mother, my sister Sonya, and I were evicted from our duplex apartment. My sister Rhonda had already moved back in with my grandparents out in the boonies, and the rest of us were forced to move in with a family friend until my mother figured out what she was going to do. I didn't know the particulars of why we were evicted, but I always knew we were struggling financially and were behind on rent.

Even though we were living with a family friend, I assumed my mother would get back on her feet eventually and we'd move somewhere else in the neighborhood; however, within a few weeks my mother decided to leave Bakersfield and move back to San Diego. My sister Rhonda would remain in Bakersfield with my grandparents so she could finish high school, and my sister Sonya and I would go back to San Diego with my mother.

CHAPTER 3

Prep School for Street Life

WE ARRIVED BACK in San Diego sometime in early 1981 and settled in a neighborhood that was notorious for gangs and crime. Although the main street that ran through the neighborhood was Ocean View Boulevard, the name couldn't have been more misleading. There was no ocean in sight. The only view I recall ever having was looking down from our upstairs two-bedroom apartment at drug addicts, drug dealers, and gang members. This era was before the crack cocaine epidemic,* and the most popular drug at the time besides marijuana was PCP.

Gangs had been very active in San Diego among Mexicans for decades, but Crips and Bloods had been around only since the early to mid-1970s. By 1981, Southeast San Diego's gang scene had exploded, and the usual gang brawls with fists, knives, golf clubs, and bats had significantly escalated into gunfights and murder. Ocean View Boulevard and T Street where I lived was smack in the middle of most of it. Just walking to the corner store would be a mini adventure. Seeing guys shooting dice, watching dozens of guys make drug deals, music blasting from every other home and car, and not to mention the gang activity, made my new environment look like every ghetto stereotype imaginable without any exaggeration.

DON'T LET YOUR PAST HOLD YOU BACK

My mother allowed me to hang out with my sisters' boyfriends in Bakersfield sometimes, and I assume she knew some of them were gang members. However, when we moved back to San Diego and I was a preteen, she seemed determined to keep me out of gangs and away from criminal activity. I think when we returned to San Diego and moved on Ocean View Boulevard, she thought I was more susceptible to the streets and she became more proactive with keeping me out of trouble. However, I don't think she realized how much I had already become accustomed to the street life while we were still in Bakersfield.

I was now eleven going on twelve and living in a neighborhood that was twice as rough as the one we lived in while in Bakersfield. Ocean View was a very fast-paced area in Southeast San Diego and was a notorious Blood neighborhood called 5/9 Brims. It felt like it was lightning-speed faster than Bakersfield. Even though I had become a regular alcohol drinker and weed smoker and was well acquainted with gang culture and other criminal elements in the neighborhood, I still wasn't involved in any criminal activity myself. I give my mother a lot of credit for refusing to allow me to get out of control early on. My mother really started to have a hold on me and my activities around this time, and she kept me in check. I guess she still looked at me as her Little Man, the nickname she had used for me since I was a baby.

Not being involved in crime or being a gang member didn't stop me from being tested every day. After moving to Ocean View Boulevard I almost immediately started getting tested by the other neighborhood boys. I was the new kid on the block, and they wanted to know who I was and how tough I was. I was always a skinny, short kid and was never known for being a great fighter, so I was definitely an easy target. I was either going to get bullied or learn how to fight or at least show that I will fight.

There's always that one kid who will be the first to challenge the new kid on the block, and for me that was Fat James. Fat James was around a year older than me. He was attending Memorial Junior High School, and I was still in the sixth grade attending Stockton Elementary. Fat James had two older brothers who were active gang members in the neighborhood and his family was well known. Every time Fat James saw me walking home from school or playing outside with the other kids in the neighborhood, he would talk trash to me and try to instigate a fight. Fat James was twice my size, a very husky kid, and although I had never seen Fat James fight, he had a reputation and there are those you don't want to test, and Fat James was definitely one of them.

For my first few months in the neighborhood Fat James talked trash to me every time he saw me. He continually tried to pick a fight with me for no apparent reason other than I was new in the neighborhood or maybe it was because I had a cool walk or both. Finally after putting up with his insults and challenges, I decided that if Fat James says anything else disrespectful to me again and gets in my face, I am going to fight him. And that's exactly what happened one day as I was walking to my friend Roy's house.

It was a Saturday morning, and although I was hoping I didn't run into Fat James, I knew that my friend Roy lived a few houses across the street from him. It was still early in the morning, and I wasn't anticipating many people to be outside, especially Fat James, the bully. As I was walking past Fat James's house on the other side of the street on my way to Roy's house, I could see Fat James out of the corner of my eye. I tried not to look his way, but soon he was in my face talking trash as usual. He started challenging me to a fight right across the street from his house and a few houses from Roy's. I kept repeating to myself in my head that I was not afraid and that I was going to hit him as hard as I could if he got too close. As soon as Fat James got close enough, I hit him as hard as I could, and then he commenced

19

to whooping my ass. All I remember is Fat James being on top of me pounding me blow after blow. He may have been fat, but he was quick as hell and after I hit him the first time, he pounced me so fast I was only able to hit him maybe a couple more times before he sat on top of me and hit me like twenty times.

After about thirty seconds of Fat James kicking my ass, I could hear his mother screaming and telling him to stop and get off of me. I could see Fat James's mother running toward us, and all I could think was, "Lady, please hurry up and get your big-ass son off of me." She eventually pulled Fat James off of me, and I got up, brushed myself off, and continued on my walk to Roy's house. To add insult to injury, when I got to Roy's house his mother told me he wasn't home. I got my ass whooped for nothing that morning.

I guess there is some truth to that saying if you stand up to bullies they will respect you, because after that fight Fat James and I became good friends. He even taught me how to shoot dice using leaves from a tree as our money. I will never dispute the fact that Fat James gave me a good whoopin', but I did stand up to him, and he respected me for it. Where I grew up if you didn't fight, whether you knew how to or not, you might as well never come outside, and I wasn't one to stay in the house.

Although I wasn't committing crimes yet and wasn't a gang member, I was far from a good boy when I was twelve years old. I was still in boot camp waiting to graduate and serve the streets instead of my country. Things would change as soon as I became a teenager. The streets had already been calling me for several years, but by then I was ready to meet them halfway. The calls became overwhelming by the time I was thirteen years old. It was becoming evident that I wouldn't be able to resist the streets much longer. My mother, on the other hand, continued her refusal to allow me to participate in any gang or criminal activities, although she occasionally allowed me to drink beer in the house. What she didn't know was I had been getting drunk almost every day since I was eleven.

Although my mother would not allow me to smoke weed, I'm sure she had her suspicions that I was smoking weed when I wasn't home. She caught me high after I came home one day with eyes bloodshot red. I tried to avoid eye contact with her, but she was suspicious because I made it too obvious that I was trying to avoid her. She demanded that I look at her, and she knew instantly that I was high. She cussed me out and told me never to do it again. I said okay and went to my room. Of course my never doing it again lasted probably until the next day or so. I had no intentions of stopping, even though smoking weed was never really a special thrill for me. I just did it because that's what we all did. Alcohol, on the other hand, was the thing that I enjoyed.

Even though my mother let me drink beer sometimes at home, she didn't allow me to hang out with guys she even suspected of being gang members, so everything I did when I was in my early teens concerning getting high or hanging out with gang members, I had to sneak and do it without my mother's knowledge.

I didn't appreciate my mother's strictness at the time. I hated her being strict, but when I became an adult, I had a lot of respect for my mother for doing her best to keep me in check during those early teen years and it made a huge difference, not only back then but later in my life. My mother's strictness in comparison to other parents in the neighborhood definitely helped keep me out of trouble for as long as it did, in stark contrast to most of my friends whose mothers either didn't care what they did or didn't know how to prevent their sons from doing whatever they wanted to do.

Most of our mothers in my neighborhood were single parents on public assistance and trying to make the best out of what limited resources they had, but my mother was not going to allow me to disrespect her in her presence, regardless of our circumstance. And I never did, even though I had friends who cussed out their mothers or talked back to them. These were guys my age at the time, thirteen years old, telling their mothers to go to hell and worse, things I wouldn't even think about saying to my mother without fear of getting slapped or hit over the head with a broomstick. I was never a model son, but I always respected my mother for the fact that she was a single parent and was struggling to raise my sisters and me the best she could. I also had sympathy for her, considering my father had left and remarried and my mother was alone. Even with her shortcomings as a parent, I always thought of my mother as my queen and appreciate her more today than I ever did.

I was now thirteen years old and still living on Ocean View Boulevard, my sister Rhonda moved back from Bakersfield to live with us fulltime before she graduated high school. I guess she couldn't take it any longer living in the boondocks with my grandparents. I remember being the only male in the house with three females: two teenage girls and my mother. At times it was overwhelming for me and I had to hang out in my room for hours or leave, but I knew I had to be the man of the house, and I loved my mother and sisters and would protect them at all costs.

Getting into fist fights with one of my mother's boyfriends or one of my sisters' boyfriends was not out of the ordinary for me. It didn't happen a lot, but it occurred from time to time. Some guys figured that my sisters or my mother had no man around to protect them so they could take advantage of that. I was only thirteen, but I was a young man, from the hood, and would get violent if I had to protect my family. Anyone who challenged that fact did so at their own peril.

The few times I did have to fight for my mother or sisters was because one of their boyfriends tried to hit them or argued with them in a menacing way that I felt was getting too close to being physical. I pounced with my fists, a bat, or a four-inch-thick and four-foot-long pipe I kept for protection. Fortunately nothing ever got too out of hand and no one was ever seriously hurt, but the message was clear: if you mess with someone in this house you'd better be ready for a fight.

Sometimes I think back and laugh at how that skinny thirteen-year-old kid who wasn't a great fighter and wasn't tough was trying to fight grown men. It was difficult being the only male in the house at such a young age, especially in an environment such as Southeast San Diego, but I will say it was great preparation for what I would face a few years later in the violent world of gangbanging and drug dealing.

I remember I occasionally daydreamed about my mother dating a man who would marry her and he would take on the role as the man of the house and be a father figure for my sisters and me, and I could just be a kid. I used think about how great it would be to have a male figure in the house to teach me regular boy stuff like playing sports and how to treat a girl instead of thinking every female who was not my mother or sister was a bitch. I'm sure many of my friends at the time had the same dreams but would never say it out loud at the risk of being perceived soft. The reality was that nothing in my dream was a real option for me, but I did have dreams and hopes of a better life during this time.

One of the biggest misconceptions about people who grow up in the ghetto is that somehow they chose to live there, but in reality they usually have no choice. Some people may be predisposed to crime, but most people are not born gangsters or criminals. Most people, even those in the inner city, have dreams or aspire to a better life outside their present circumstances. Sure, my friends and I knew right from wrong, and no one ever put a gun to our heads and forced us to join a gang or break the law, but for many people being in a gang and being involved in criminal activity in the inner city is more of a way of life than something you sit down and write out as a goal you aspire to when you grow up. When you're a child you are forced to live wherever your parents or guardians put you. And then it becomes a struggle not to become a product of that environment.

By the time you become a teenager or young adult during your most impressionable and productive years, it's not usually an option to get up and move to the suburbs. Most of my friends and I were going through the same thing living on Ocean View Boulevard. This is what many black and Latino males growing up in the inner city experience. Don't get me wrong, personally there wasn't a day that went by that I didn't dream about having a life outside of my immediate environment. Unfortunately in Southern California inner-city communities, joining a gang is one of the most prominent and appealing options for many black and Latino males. Although I wasn't yet a full-fledged gang member, I was already immersed in the culture, which included a lot of crime and violence.

CHAPTER 4

Just Another Day in the Ghetto

ABOUT A YEAR after moving back to San Diego we moved from our apartment to a house a few blocks away on Millbrae Street, which was notorious for being the busiest PCP street in San Diego. It didn't take long before I witnessed several gang and drug-related stabbings and shootings. A few people I knew from around the neighborhood were murdered or seriously wounded on my street. I remember coming home one night with my mother after spending the day in Chula Vista at my Uncle Jesse and Aunt Margret's house and our entire street was blocked off with yellow tape. The police wouldn't let any cars through, so we had to go all the way around the block just to get home. Once we got home and started talking to everyone standing outside, we soon realized it was TC, who I knew from around the neighborhood and who also briefly dated my sister Sonya, who had gotten shot. He had been shot by some West Coast Crips, a rival gang from right over the bridge on Ocean View Boulevard. TC was only sixteen years old. After that, I remember being scared to walk down the street in broad daylight for fear of getting shot. I was only thirteen, but because of the neighborhood I lived in, my age, and who I hung around, I was considered a fair target.

I still vividly remember the night TC got shot with the ambulances out there and the police cars blocking the street. TC's death was not the first to occur on my street, but it was the first time someone I was personally acquainted with died from a gang shooting.

Most of the violence in my neighborhood was gang or drug related, with the occasional domestic dispute. Another one of my early vivid memories of street violence happened while my whole family was sitting on the porch listening to music and talking. We would have the music blasting and various people from around the neighborhood would stop and come onto the porch and hang out. Our house was one of the more popular hangout spots on the street. Most of the guys in the neighborhood wanted to date one of my sisters, so they took the opportunity for any reason to stop and chat. On this particular night as we were all sitting on the porch laughing and probably drinking, I saw a dark figure walking up the street toward my house. When he got close enough, I was able to make out who he was. He was one of the older black gang members from the neighborhood. As he approached our house about four carloads full of Mexican gang members pulled up next to him, jumped out of their cars, and attacked him. At least ten or twelve men attacked him with fists and knives. I remember him screaming for help as he was being repeatedly pummeled by the Mexican gang members. Although I was only thirteen and had some fear for my own safety, I felt a responsibility to help this guy, even though I didn't know him well. I knew who he was and I hung out occasionally with his younger brother, Pokie, who was around my age. I also felt I had an obligation to help him because he was black, and if I didn't try to do something and allowed some Mexican gang members to kill him, it was a chance I couldn't walk that neighborhood anymore. Although blacks and Mexicans coexisted in my neighborhood in harmony for the most part, there was the occasional friction and tit for tat between the two races.

I hesitated for about thirty seconds before I ran out of my yard screaming at the Mexican guys to stop. Fortunately for me my mother and sisters ran after me screaming for me to come back. I think they grabbed me and pulled me back on the porch. Although I was serious about helping the guy who was being stabbed, I doubt there was much I could have done to help him in that situation. He got stabbed up pretty badly, but he survived and fully recovered.

I would learn a few days later that the Mexican guys attacked him because of a bad drug deal and the attack wasn't racial or gang related. He could have died right in front me and in front of my house and I was cool with his little brother. But that kind of stuff always went down on Ocean View Boulevard. As they used to say, "if you're scared stay in the house or go to church."

There were other instances around the neighborhood where I heard numerous gunshots or saw someone laid out on the ground seriously injured or dead. Because of the dangerous environment I lived in it became the norm for me to carry around knives, box cutters, metal poles, golf clubs, and bats whenever I left the house. I had carried a switchblade when I was younger, but that was just for showing off. Now I was carrying weapons for my protection because at the age of thirteen, coupled with the neighborhood I was living in and the crowd I was running with, I had become a real target. If you hung out, you were fair game.

At thirteen my life had become seriously in danger every single time I walked out my front door. I had become a target just because I was a black male who was old enough to be a gang member. It didn't take long that I started being shot at or chased by gang members from other neighborhoods. It was just a matter of time before I completely gave myself to the streets.

Even with all of the negative influences around me, I did have people who came into my life occasionally and tried to encourage me to go in the right direction. My cousin Fred was one person with whom I had periodic contact who had done well for himself. He tried to encourage me to stay away from the street life. Fred owned a nice home in a nice middle-class neighborhood, and I saw him only when he came over maybe once a month. Fred knew and understood the environment I was growing up in and tried to convince me to stay out of trouble and focus on school. I would be polite and listen whenever Fred talked to me, but it was hard to appreciate what he was saying when I didn't know if I would have enough food to eat for dinner that night or whether I would be shot or stabbed the next day. I listened to what he said, but once he left I was still faced with my reality. I had more pressing things on my mind.

When I became an adult, however, I told my cousin Fred I remember and appreciated the advice he gave me.

There's something to be said about not being able to understand the path someone is walking unless you have walked on that path yourself. I learned it's always easier to give advice to people from a distance when you are not or have never been faced with their reality. Even though a number of people I came across offered me advice, I politely listened, because my mama told me to respect those senior to me, but I always went back to my reality.

One of the most memorable experiences I had with someone trying to give me some good advice happened while I was being driven home by my junior high school counselor after being suspended. Thirty-plus years later I still remember our talk on that twenty- to twenty-five-minute drive from Marston Junior High School in the neighborhood of Claremont to Southeast San Diego.

I had been bused out to Marston Junior High when I was in the eighth grade because I had got kicked out of Wilson Junior High for smoking weed, then I went to Horace Mann Junior High and got kicked out for fighting, and then my last stop was Gompers Junior High where I got expelled about a month after I got there for threatening a teacher.

This all happened while I was in the seventh grade and the school district decided there was nowhere else to send for the remaining of the school year so they put me on home-schooling and decided to bus me out to Marston in a predominately white neighborhood for the eighth grade. I don't remember why I got suspended on that day but I remember my mother didn't have a car to drive all the way to Marston to pick me up, so my school counselor drove me home.

My counselor was aware that I had been expelled from three schools in the prior school year and he was also aware that I had started getting into trouble at Marston. He was also aware that I lived in a rough neighborhood in Southeast San Diego. Once he and I got into his car, he asked me a number of questions, such as what did I want to be when I grew up and did I play any sports. It was a typical small-talk conversation, and surprisingly he wasn't being overly preachy or scolding me about getting suspended. As we got closer to downtown San Diego and looked at the skyline from his car on Interstate 5 on our way to Southeast, my counselor looked over at me and said something I would never forget. I'm paraphrasing but as he pointed to the high rise buildings in downtown, he said, "Do you see those buildings over there?" I nodded my head in the affirmative.

"The real gangsters are in those buildings." He then said to me, "If you want to be a gangster, you should aspire to be one of those gangsters."

I was only thirteen years old at the time, but what he said has stayed with me all these years. I didn't understand the significance of what he was trying to tell me until I was much older. It wasn't until I became an adult and was sitting in federal prison with former doctors, lawyers, judges, politicians, corporate executives, and other professionals who were once at the top of their profession, that the light would come on like an epiphany, and I knew exactly what my counselor was trying to tell me all those years ago. It became even clearer once I started working in corporate America myself. The real gangsters are the movers and shakers of the world, not some hood rich guy in the ghetto who everyone looks up to. What my counselor told me back in 1983 stayed with me even though it took many years to completely embrace. I don't remember his name or what happened to him. All I remember is he was Latino, probably in his twenties. If I ever see him again, I will thank him for caring and then let him know that his words were not in vain and had a positive impact on my life, albeit not until many years later.

Back in the early 1980s, anything that could have possibly had a positive influence on me and changed the trajectory of my life went over my head or never came into my existence. Gangs and crime were a way of life, and I couldn't see any other way. As challenging as my Ocean View Boulevard experience was, it was just a precursor to what I was about to experience during the crack epidemic on the Four Corners of Death.

CHAPTER 5

The Four Corners of Death

THERE ARE CERTAIN areas in San Diego that are infamous only to the locals. If you grew up in Southeast or East Dago, even if you have been away from the city for more than twenty-five years, you still remember the Four Corners of Death.*

The Four Corners of Death had a number of rival gangs within five or ten minutes of the intersection. In the heart of the Four Corners was Ghost Town Crips. Ghost Town was one of only two Crip gangs in the vicinity surrounded by Bloods on each side. The other Crip gang was the Rollin Neighborhood 40s Crips. There was Lil Africa Piru and Emerald Hills Bloods a few blocks north of Ghost Town. You had the Skyline Pirus and O'Farrell Park Bangster Bloods farther to the east of the Four Corners. And the closest and biggest Blood gang to the Four Corners was the Lincoln Park Bloods. The Blood gangs didn't always get along, so that made this area even more dangerous. During the crack epidemic to say the Four Corners of Death was dangerous would be an understatement. As we would say, it was "hot."

Although law enforcement and other city officials would like to deny its existence or diminish its infamous reputation, this particular area at the intersection of Imperial and Euclid Avenues was synonymous with gang warfare and drug dealing back in the 1980s and early

1990s. The Four Corners was a major intersection in Southeast San Diego, and a number of gang members from all over the city could be in the intersection at any time and collide with each other. It was like a suicide mission just to get out of your car in the parking lot of Greene Cat Liquor Store, pumping gas at the Shell gas station, standing at the Taco Shop waiting for food, or coming out of Huffman's Barbeque, if you had any street reputation. In fact just driving and stopping at the red light on Euclid and Imperial could be your last day on earth.

For me the Four Corners of Death was more up close and personal than for most people. After leaving Ocean View Boulevard, we moved into an apartment complex directly adjacent to Greene Cat Liquor Store, which was on the corner of Imperial and Euclid Avenues. There were a number of apartment complexes near the Four Corners of Death, but I lived in the ones right on it. This was around 1984, and the crack epidemic was just beginning to explode in San Diego, and I was living right in the middle of one of the major hubs of drug dealing and gangbanging. I can say it now without feeling like a snitch, but more drug deals were made at the Shell gas station back in the day than just about anywhere in Southeast San Diego. I know because I made a lot of them and saw many more.

Initially, I hadn't begun selling drugs when we moved to the Four Corners, although surrounded by the temptation like never before. When I lived on Ocean View, the drugs of choice were PCP and marijuana, and no one my age was making a lot of money from them, and certainly not getting rich. But, in and around my apartment complex on the Four Corners, I could see the instant gratification and overnight success of drug dealers not much older than me.

By the time 1985 came, it seemed like everyone was either addicted to crack or trying to become rich off of crack, and when I say "everyone," that's no exaggeration. Of course there were people who didn't partake in the crack epidemic, but from my perspective it sure seemed like everyone was involved. For sure there were a lot of hardworking, working-class people who despised what was going on in the community, and I knew that to be the case, but when the epidemic hit, it was so profound that it came like a category five hurricane without any warning. For me it was as if one day everyone my age was either gangbanging or selling weed or PCP and then boom, they were either addicted to this horrible drug called crack or getting rich off of it. It wasn't unusual to see someone who just six months prior had no money and was taking public transportation to get around the city, and then you would see this same person now driving around town in a Cadillac or an El Camino or a Nissan Truck with a three-thousand-dollar candy paint job and two-thousand-dollar Dayton Wire wheels. It started to become the norm to see overnight success stories drug dealer. The Four Corners would turn into a car show in an instant at the Shell gas station or in front of Huffman's Barbeque. I was only fourteen or fifteen at the time and was still scared to even think about selling drugs, but I was fascinated by the nice cars, the fancy Turkish ropes and other jewelry, and most of all the pretty girls that seemed always to accompany one of the rich drug dealers.

My apartment complex on the Four Corners was a major crack spot, even though my particular apartment was not at the time. I would say out of the fifteen apartment units where I lived, at least five of them were crack houses, not including the duplex right across the alley where the Cuban drug mobster, Victor, lived. Victor was a big-time drug dealer from Miami who had set up shop right across the alley from my apartments. I don't recall there ever being any major drug war in my apartment complex, considering all of the competition. I guess the money was plentiful, and as long as you didn't get caught shortstopping, which means stealing customers from another drug dealer on their turf, everything was kosher. That doesn't mean there were not a lot of fights and shootings, but most of them were between drug addicts or gang members. Living in the middle of all this action in a crammed, roach-infested two-bedroom apartment with my mother, my two sisters, and my niece, I could not remain a spectator for too much longer.

Back in the 1980s Southeast San Diego had four major high schools: Lincoln, Morse, San Diego, and Mt. Miguel. If you wanted to include the two other main high schools in East Dago, you also had Hoover and Crawford. I attended Lincoln High School for my freshman and sophomore years while living on the Four Corners. Lincoln was a short distance from where I lived right down Imperial Avenue. Lincoln High had always been a relatively good school academically and was well known for its athletics. There were always good teachers and gifted students, but one of my most prominent memories was its gang culture. This probably can be said about most of the high schools in Southeast and East Dago. In the 1980s it was common to see rival gang fights on school campus in addition to regular fights between people who had no gang affiliation. The gang fights at Lincoln were not limited to between Crips against Bloods, but instead a lot of the fighting would be between different Blood gangs or Mexican gangs. The fights would occur before, during, or after school.

The gang culture was so prevalent during this time that most of the teachers at Lincoln High School assumed many of their students were involved in gangs and could potentially become victims of its violence. One of the saddest examples of this occurred during the week right before my summer break in the ninth grade. I was in detention like I usually was at least once a month for either getting caught ditching class or doing something else. On this particular day we had detention with Mr. Polk, who was not only the detention teacher but also the basketball coach. I was in there with several other students, including my friend Hess-Dogg, who was a member of Ghost Town Crips. Hess-Dogg and I were in the back of the class joking around like we normally did, not taking anyone or anything seriously, when

Mr. Polk started giving the class one of his usual lectures about school and life. Mr. Polk was very familiar with the problems of gangs not only in the school but also in the community, and he would occasionally give us an anti-gang motivational talk. Of course to us it was more like a sermon than any motivational speech, because we were so hardheaded. I had gotten this talk from Mr. Polk many times before, but on this particular day it would turn out to be one of his most ominous and memorable talks ever. I recall Mr. Polk's words to all of us in that classroom as though I am hearing him say them today. At the very end of his usual lecture he said, "Some of you in this class today won't survive this summer and make it back to school next year." What he was alluding to, and rightly so, was the odds were that at least one of us in that classroom would probably be murdered over the summer. I didn't give what Mr. Polk said much thought at the time. I was too busy in the back of the classroom goofing off with Hess-Dogg and several others, just waiting for the bell to ring so we could leave. I don't recall if it was our final period of the day, but I do know we were eager to leave. In hindsight we weren't really being disrespectful to Mr. Polk by not taking him seriously. We respected him. It's just when you're stuck in your environment and people tell you to avoid certain things, when you're living them every day from the time you wake up in the morning until the time you go to bed and in between, even at school, it's hard to sit back and really think about what they're saying. We were still stuck in poverty and were children, so there was no option to escape our current circumstances. We had become numb to statements like the ones Mr. Polk made, however, his statements on that particular day would still haunt me to this very day.

It was just another summer night hanging out in front of my apartment complex on the Four Corners of Death. Typically on warm summer nights everyone would be outside and there would be music playing and a barbeque grill cooking. That may sound country or ghetto to some people, but hey, that was how we enjoyed a warm summer night. The scene would sometimes be like a block party, but instead it was just the whole apartment complex and a few visitors.

Initially there was nothing particularly unusual about this night. I had gone next door to Green Cat Liquor store to buy something and that's where I ran into Hess-Dogg. We chatted for a few minutes before he headed back down to Groveland Street where most of the Ghost Town Crips hung out. I went back to my apartment and continued to post up with my neighbors outside. I don't recall what Hess-Dogg and I had discussed that night but usually whenever we ran into each other it was small talk. He was from that neighborhood and I had just moved over there so we saw each other often even when we weren't at school. Hess-Dogg and couple of his homies like Ace and Lil Bossie would sometimes shoot dice and smoke weed with me in front of my apartments. I was also cool with Gaylon who was an OG from Ghost Town, because he was dating my sister Sonya's friend, Gina. And my family grew up with the founder of Ghost Town, Big Boo Hines, and his siblings.

However, my time on the Four Corners, and Ghost Town in particular, started off with drama. When I first moved over there I had heard that someone told some members of Ghost Town I had just moved from Ocean View and they had inquired about whether I was gangbanging or not. One day I was walking home and out of nowhere I was approached by several Ghost Town members. Before I could utter one word or knew what was happening I was hit and on the ground. I got up off the ground then ran home and told my neighbor who was standing outside that some Ghost Town Crips just rushed me. She and her boyfriend ran one of the main crack houses in the apartment complex. After I explained to her what happened, she immediately went in the house and came back with a handgun and then handed it to me.

After my neighbor gave me the gun, I told my sisters what happened.

Then my neighbor. Then her boyfriend. Then my sisters, and I, all went down the alley to confront about ten Ghost Town Crips who were waiting on us. I was only fourteen years old and had never shot anybody. In fact I hadn't held too many guns at this point in my life. But I wasn't scared and my adrenaline forced me to keep walking down the alley though I knew the dudes from Ghost Town had guns too, and they were killers.

Eventually someone in our group suggested, and rightly so, that we turn around a go back to our apartments. We did. About five minutes later some of the dudes from Ghost Town came to our apartment and threw bricks through our living room and kitchen windows shattering them both. Right after that we called Big Boo Hines and he immediately came over and first talked to me and my family. Then he talked to Ghost Town and put an end to the feud. I was safe from any further attack from Ghost Town, but Big Boo Hines couldn't guarantee my safety from anyone else and remember, this was the Four Corners of Death in the 1980s.

After I talked to Hess-Dogg that night, maybe a couple of hours or so later, I heard a succession of gunshots coming from the direction of Groveland Street which was a few blocks away. I wasn't surprised to hear gunshots, considering that whole area was inundated with gangs and drugs. Hearing gunshots wasn't unusual so I didn't think twice about it until a few minutes later when I heard sirens. What seemed like only ten minutes after hearing the gunshots, I watched as a helicopter flew over. Gunshots followed by sirens were also not unusual in the heart of gang capital of San Diego. But seeing a helicopter continue to hover over and get lower and lower was definitely something I wasn't familiar with. Within a few minutes the helicopter landed in the middle of a residential area. I had never seen anything like that before. I waited in front of my apartment complex hoping someone would come by and tell me what happened.

Within minutes several people came walking through the alley and told us that someone had been shot. We had already assumed that, but I wanted to know how serious it was and who it was. Over the hours more information started to come in about the shooting, and the initial rumor was that it had been a shootout between some Crips and Bloods on Groveland Street. At this point I still didn't know who got shot. I wouldn't find out until later that night that the helicopter turned out to be a Life Flight from the hospital's trauma center and had escorted the gravely injured patient via helicopter ambulance back to the hospital. I found out that the person who was shot was Hess-Dogg. He died from his injuries that night.

For the rest of the night and into the morning all I could think about was what Mr. Polk told us during detention. He said one of us in that room would not make it through the summer. What made it even more eerie in addition to remembering what Mr. Polk said, I had just talked to Hess-Dogg earlier that night. He was only sixteen years old with his whole life ahead of him. What was so ironic about his death, Hess-Dogg was loved by both sides, Crips and Bloods. But that's how it was in the hood it's always the cool ones who get caught in the crossfire. I wish that would have been my last time experiencing a close friend dying tragically from gang and gun violence, but unfortunately it would be many more to come.

By 1985 my particular apartment complex on the Four Corners was increasingly becoming one of the biggest crack cocaine bazaars in the city. I guesstimate that at least ten thousand dollars in drug money exchanged hands in my apartment complex each day, and likely much more if you include Cuban Victor across the alley.

Although I admit I was giving into the street life more and more each day and had already been well acquainted with gang life since my days in Bakersfield. I was still afraid to sell crack cocaine. I had sold a little weed every now and then but the thought of selling cocaine terrified me. I was only fifteen years old and I knew selling crack was serious business and I didn't think I was ready for it. Almost everyone around me smoked weed, and it seemed like a harmless drug to your health and at best a petty crime to smoke or sell it. Crack cocaine, however, was a different story.

With my own eyes, I witnessed the violence that crack cocaine could bring to someone's life. Drug dealers beating up crack addicts over unpaid debts or stolen drugs. Crack dealers being robbed. Drug wars between various groups over territory. And the most devastating of all for me was watching crack cocaine destroy people I looked up to even people in my own family. But there's often something that brings you to the point where your fears are outweighed by a stronger desire. The fear of disappointing my mother, being incarcerated, or being physically harmed or murdered were finally outweighed by a desire to make money.

At this point I had experienced poverty on and off since I was eight years old. I was tired of being broke. I was tired of struggling. I was even tired of my family being broke. I was tired of wearing last year's styles. Pro Wings shoes and Toughskin jeans just wasn't cutting it anymore. I was tired of eating the same pot of pinto beans for breakfast, lunch, and dinner for a week. I was in high school now and it mattered more than ever before how I presented myself. I knew the risks, but as my homie, DJL aka Lil CS, would say, "I'd rather live a short rich life than a long poor life." In fact, that saying would become one of my mantras that would justify many of my subsequent risks.

Selling crack cocaine, especially on the Four Corners, was a way of life and it finally seeped into my home. I started to suspect one of my sisters as well as my mother of using crack. It seemed like everyone around me was either selling crack or using it. The final straw was watching my classmates who just a few weeks earlier were regular guys just like me but now coming to school flashing hundreds of dollars in class and bragging about how much money they made the night before. Except for maybe a few, most of my friends had already started selling crack. I noticed that they started wearing expensive name brand clothes and jewelry such as large Turkish rope gold chains which was the jewelry of choice for most crack dealers. People my age and from my neighborhood were earning hundreds if not thousands of dollars in one night. My decision to sell crack was no longer difficult.

I was terrified of crack cocaine because I knew its power over people, but I couldn't resist its allure any longer and began selling it at age fifteen. I got my first bag of crack cocaine on consignment, which was typically how many people got started. Although my neighborhood and apartment complex were a paradise for crack dealers and users alike, I didn't have any clientele for when I started off and the competition was fierce for street corner drug dealers like me. There was no shortage of young crack dealers ready to live their ghetto dreams and become the next crack cocaine kingpin. During this time the supply was limitless and so was the demand. Unless you had a connection with someone who was already connected with a significant amount of drugs and could set you up in a crack house, you typically started off on a street corner as a smalltime dealer competing with a dozen or so other people.

Initially I never made more than a few hundred dollars over a couple of days and usually most of that went to the person I was working for and I spent the rest on food and clothes. But that didn't matter to me around this time. I was just happy to finally have money in my pocket and not have to worry about whether I would have enough food to eat that night or have to eat the same leftovers for several days in a row. I also could finally go to the mall and buy nice clothes and nice shoes. My days of Pro Wings and Toughskins were over. In fact, this was the first time in my life that I could wear name brand attire and not feel embarrassed about going to school with holes in my Pro Wing tennis shoes and ragged Toughskin jeans. I admit, though I knew selling crack was contributing to the demise of my community and was a very dangerous lifestyle, it felt really good not to feel poor anymore. I make no apologies for what I believed at the time I needed to do to improve my situation. I do have serious regrets. I own my past.

To improve my living situation, I believed my options were limited to selling drugs. I didn't play sports, nor was I a good student academically or citizenship wise, so I knew college was not in the pipeline. No one ever sat me down and seriously discussed any trade I could learn that would lead to a career opportunity after high school.

My father had been in the Navy and both of my brothers were serving in the Navy. Most people I knew joined the military because the court gave them the option instead of facing incarceration. I was fifteen years old, a small time drug dealer, and wannabe gangster. I started thinking about my future as an adult and doing something productive with my life. I considered the military as an option and enrolled in J.R.O.T.C. for a couple of semesters while I was still at Lincoln High. Since my father and my brothers and been in the Navy and were doing well for themselves, it was definitely something worth thinking about. However, the allure of fast money and instant success was overwhelming. I'd been living on public assistance and had been poor for the previous eight years with no obvious talents or skills. I just didn't see any realistic long-term goal for myself besides becoming the biggest drug dealer I could become. When I watched other guys I was going to school with become rich overnight while I still struggled without many of life's basic necessities, selling crack was a no brainer. It didn't take long before I dropped out of J.R.O.T.C. and gave up any thought of ever going into the military.

As we used to say, "It was on and crackin'," and I meant that literally. Once I got a taste of making fast money, listening to my mother or teachers, or even dreaming of a life beyond drug dealing and gang violence were all quickly becoming things of the past. I was fifteen years old, and like any other fifteen year old, it was all about hanging out with friends and having fun. My hanging out on Ocean View consisted mostly of getting high, now it was getting money first and finding some time in between to get high.

The crack cocaine epidemic and the Southern California gang culture in the 1980s were so entrenched in my everyday existence it quickly became the only future I envisioned for myself, and there was no better place to be for this kind of thinking than on the Four Corners of Death.

It was around the summer of 1985, and EJ, who was a good friend of the family and like an uncle to me, took me under his wing. I had known EJ since my days on Ocean View where he was some kind of community leader organizing all of the break dancing competitions at Ocean View Park. He always had an energetic personality and was very affable. When my family and I moved to the Four Corners, EJ had become a drug dealer, like a lot of people during the crack cocaine scene. I was almost sixteen, and EJ was already in his late twenties or early thirties. It wasn't long before I realized EJ was somewhat of a big drug dealer. The apartment complex I lived in was one of the major crack scenes, and EJ would do business with several of the crack houses in the complex and then visit my family and me after his business. Since EJ was such a close person to our family and had such a likable personality, my mother and my sisters trusted him. It wasn't long before EJ started taking me out of town with him during the summer after my tenth grade to distribute drugs. He was working for a big-time drug dealer out of Los Angeles named Tyrone. EJ would take me with him to Tyrone's house in Pomona to pick up the drugs prior to our going on our trip to various cities within Riverside and San Bernardino counties to set up crack houses. We would stay in each city for a few days and have people sell the crack. We would then collect the money and move on to the next city. After a week or two of selling drugs, we would head back to Tyrone's in Pomona and drop off the money and then head down to San Diego. We would stay in San Diego for about three or four days and then head back out of town and repeat the whole process again. We did this for most of the summer. I was basically there to watch EJ's back and help him out with miscellaneous things such as count money, safe guard and stash drugs, and assist him with distributing drugs to clients. I guess you could say I was his executive assistant. He knew I was from the streets and would have his back if anything ever happened.

I had just recently started selling crack before I started working with EJ. I had been looking up to other big-time drug dealers in my neighborhood for at least a year. I knew several of them in passing. However, I hadn't known any high-level drug dealers until EJ started coming around.

A lot of my peers were hood rich and worth thousands of dollars, which was a lot of money for someone in high school who was recently broke. To be friends with people like EJ and then able to rub elbows with Tyrone, a bigtime money-making drug dealer or baller as we called them back then, I felt like my dope dealing dreams were finally coming to fruition.

Whenever I went to Tyrone's house I would be treated like a little brother because I was younger than everyone else. We would usually spend the night at Tyrone's on the first night before heading out to Riverside and San Bernardino Counties.

Tyrone lived in a huge house in a gated community in a suburban neighborhood of Pomona, California. Tyrone, like most ballers, had a beautiful wife. She was "bad," and when I say bad, she was bad in a very good way, with a fine caramel colored gorgeous face and a banging body to go with it. She would make any man drool especially a teenage boy. Back then drug dealers were like jocks that got the pretty girls, and among making money that was another of my attractions to the profession. Tyrone also had a cute daughter who was a toddler. There were always a number of fancy cars in Tyrone's driveway, including a Mercedes and BMW. He also always wore lots of jewelry, particular the big gold Turkish ropes that were popular with drug dealers from Southern California at the time. Tyrone seemed to have everything an impressionable young drug dealer from the hood aspired to attain: a lot of money and material possessions, a gorgeous woman on his side, and power and respect in the streets.

EJ had a great system of doing business, and he was very smart. He didn't drink alcohol, nor did he ever use drugs. Also I believe he was a graduate of San Diego State University. EJ definitely wasn't the usual drug dealer from my neighborhood or any inner city of the time. I believe Tyrone knew EJ was really smart, and that's why he trusted him with such a large amount of drugs and money.

EJ was not flashy like other drug dealers. You couldn't tell he made a lot of money or was even a drug dealer, if you didn't know better. My experience working for EJ that summer further enhanced my desire to make fast money. A seed was planted being around him and Tyrone. After that summer, even if I had to risk losing my life or my freedom for life, it was all about the money. It would be another year or so before I'd actually hear the saying and embrace it, "I would rather live a short rich life than a long poor life."

There I was back in the slum apartment complex on the Four Corners of Death after spending a summer going to Tyrone's spacious house and experiencing his suburban neighborhood and other luxuries foreign to my everyday reality.

After that summer I would occasionally sell drugs for EJ in San Diego, but for the most part I did my own thing. EJ eventually stopped coming around The Fourth Corners, and I wouldn't run into him again until a couple of years later.

My days on the Four Corners of Death during the mid-1980s were like playing tag with Satan. Any inner city can be rough, but this was a very dangerous time and place for any black male, young or old. Surrounded by five or six different gangs who all were warring with each other at any time, and coupled with everyone vying for drug turfs, not to mention my time out of town setting up numerous crack houses with EJ, it's almost a miracle I made it to my sixteen birthday. Don't get me wrong; there were a lot of close calls, but somehow I managed to stay in one piece. It wouldn't be long before I would start carrying a gun regularly around the neighborhood and even to school. It was a really dangerous place, and I knew if I didn't have protection it would be just a matter of time before my mother would have to bury me.

I had just turned sixteen, and it was the first time I ever started carrying around a loaded gun. I had carried guns with me on a couple of occasions before, but they were never loaded. Back when I used to go out of town with EJ, he would always bring guns with us, but I rarely touched them or was personally involved in one being used. I wasn't a gangsta yet and definitely not a gunslinger. However, there were two occasions where I witnessed EJ pull out a gun on someone. The first occurred when EJ and I were on our way back to San Diego from Riverside on Interstate 15 and had a road-rage incident with another vehicle. Guns were drawn in both cars while going seventy miles an hour, but fortunately the other car got off at the next exit and EJ and I continued on the freeway. Then there was the time EJ pulled a gun on a crack dealer while we were in a crack house in Banning, California. The drug dealer owed EJ money. EJ and the guy started arguing. I was instructed by EJ to get his gun from the kitchen. This was the first time I ever saw someone have a loaded gun put to their head, but it definitely wouldn't be the last time. Once I returned with EJ's gun and handed it to him, EJ cornered the guy and threw him on the floor with the gun to the guy's head. He was begging for his life. I was terrified and didn't want to witness EJ kill someone, so I went into bathroom. Fortunately for the guy, EJ let him go and I didn't have to experience someone getting shot in the next room. I never knew if EJ was seriously going to shoot the guy, but he had a good laugh at my expense for going into the bathroom. I was probably just as scared as the guy with the gun being held to his head. EJ would never let me forget it. What's so strange about that episode is that I was terrified at the time at the thought of being in the next room with someone getting shot, but ironically about a year or so later I would earn the nickname Gunsmoke. It's strange how one's environment can change them so dramatically in such a short period of time.

When you're from the streets, that terrifying feeling of possessing a gun goes away real fast when you are shot at multiple times or hear about your close friends or acquaintances getting murdered. After you have held a loaded gun several times, it becomes a way of life.

To be honest, at the time I didn't particularly enjoy guns, nor was I afraid of getting arrested for possessing one. I didn't give it much thought. My thinking was I'd rather get caught by the police with a gun than caught by an enemy without one. I had been hearing about or witnessing gang- and drug-related shootings since my days on Ocean View Boulevard. Now that I was getting older and living at the Four Corners of Death, I was becoming more and more a target. That's just how it was back then. If you were a black or brown male, once you looked a certain age, you were fair game and everyone assumed you were an active gang member. I was also becoming increasingly more involved in selling drugs, and even though I still went to school, I was dedicating my life to the streets more and more each day. In fact, my time at the Four Corners of Death was just training for what I was about to experience on 44th Street in East Dago.

Rest in Heaven, Hess Dogg.

The Four Corners of Death

CHAPTER 6

Initiation of a Mobsta

ALTHOUGH I HAD already become well acquainted with street life from my days in Bakersfield and then living in Southeast San Diego, East Dago is where I came into my own as a drug dealer and gang member. It wasn't until I moved to East Dago did I start selling drugs on a consistent basis and began earning a formidable reputation as a gang member. My best friend Dave, whom most homies called Chippy or Chippy Dave, had also just moved to East Dago from the Four Corners of Death. I first met Dave when we both lived off of Ocean View Boulevard, where we used to break dance every day after school. He and his brothers, Mike and Joey, had just moved from New York at the height of break dancing in the early 1980s, and this is where Dave and I first became acquainted. I guess it was meant for us to become best friends eventually, because it seemed like every time I moved or he moved, we ended up in the same neighborhood since we were twelve.

It was late 1986 when Dave and I both ended up in East Dago. East Dago already had a major influx of drugs as well as gang activity. Its official name back then was East San Diego, but everyone called it East Dago. East San Diego's name was officially changed to City Heights. However, it will always be considered East Dago to the people who grew up there and to the locals throughout Southeast.

My mother, my sisters Sonya and Rhonda, and I all moved into an apartment on 44th Street between the streets of Landis and Wightman directly across from the infamous Highland Park. East Dago was about a ten-minute drive from the Four Corners of Death and was not considered Southeast San Diego, but it had the same gang activity, illegal drugs, and crime. In fact, East Dago in the mid and late 1980s was an ideal location for a crack dealer with aspirations of becoming rich. The area had multiple low- to moderate-income apartment complexes stretching for about a dozen or so blocks, which made the potential number of crack houses almost limitless. I had a lot of exposure and training in dealing crack in the heart of Southeast, but when I moved to East Dago, as it relates to the streets, it was like I went from high school straight to graduate school. East Dago would catapult me to the heights of gangbanging and drug dealing that I probably never had envisioned.

Dave and I were both new to the neighborhood and would be challenged to assert and prove ourselves. We had something in common that most guys in the neighborhood didn't have; we didn't grow up in East Dago but had just as much ambition as anyone to become the biggest drug dealer and reputable gang member we could, and at any cost.

Although I was still attending high school, I was quickly becoming a full-time drug dealer and part-time student. I was never involved in school and went only because my mother made me. When I moved to East Dago, however, school became even less of a priority than before. Just like where I lived on the Four Corners of Death, 44th Street was one of the busiest drug streets in East Dago, and the particular apartments where I lived had at least two crack houses maybe more out of eight units. I can't put a precise dollar amount on the drugs that were sold on 44th Street at the peak of the crack epidemic, but crack houses lined up for about four or five blocks, and my apartment complex was one of the main locations. It's like I couldn't escape it if I really wanted to.

DON'T LET YOUR PAST HOLD YOU BACK

We've all heard the saying, "back in my day," as though some earlier era was better than the present. When it comes to gangs in Southern California or gangs in general, I won't say that it was ever better when it comes to gangbanging, because it can be extremely detrimental and destructive in any era. But unlike the late 1970s and 1980s before the internet, YouTube, Twitter, and other forms of social media, for real gang members to be taken seriously they had to earn their stripes in the streets. I'll say it anyway, back in my day people earned their reputation by having combat with so-called enemies, not posting a couple of rap videos and sending out a few threatening tweets without any real consequences in the streets.

The predominant black gang in East Dago when I moved there in late 1986 was a fledgling group consisting of guys who called themselves the East Dago Mob. The East Dago Mob at the time was relatively small in numbers in comparison to the older and much larger black gangs in Southeast San Diego. Because of its recent formation, the small amount of members, and the location of its territory that was not technically in Southeast where the more infamous gangs were located at the time, East Dago Mob members were zealously dedicated to proving themselves as official gangsters and hustlers. East Dago Mob was also different from most of other local black gangs because initially East Dago's primary focus was not gangbanging but instead making money.

When East Dago Mob was initially formed in the mid-1980s, it did not seek to have gang confrontations over colors of a bandanna or a particular neighborhood, though its colors were white and black, but it prided itself as being hustlers and money makers above everything else. East Dago **M**oney **O**ver **B**itches. Although East Dago Mob was derived from an all-Crip gang called Playboys Incorporated or PBI, once it became East Dago Mob, there were some members who originated from Southeast San Diego and were Bloods. However, by late 1988 and early 1989, when the crack cocaine epidemic was starting to fizzle out and with most of the OGs being sent either to the feds or getting long stretches of time in the state penitentiaries, East Dago Mob, without much structure and leadership remaining, would become exclusively a Crip gang and focused more on gangbanging like the other gangs in Southeast than money making. What likely contributed most to this change was the drug money started to dry up and the feds came in and sent most of the shot callers to prison. Most of those left went back to what they knew how to do best in the hood, and that was gangbanging. Money was no longer priority number one. East Dago had become no different than Southeast San Diego, except it was a few miles away.

During my day in the late 1980s, East Dago Mob would become one of the wealthiest and most powerful black gangs in San Diego. Its small numbers of members in comparison to other black gangs in Southeast made it a more tight-knit gang, as well as its massive territory of limitless apartment complexes to sell drugs. It was also far enough from the heart of Southeast and turf wars which gave its members more time to focus on making money.

Even with all of my own gangbanging fantasies, I never understood why people would actually choose gangbanging if they had another option. Back in the 1980s when I was growing up the only people who gangbanged were those living in the ghetto and who were surround-ed by poverty and despair, even if not technically poor themselves. Back in those days if you weren't a Crip you didn't Crip Walk.* Crip Walking was a dance invented by Crips and was usually only done at a house party or just hanging out with your homies in the hood let-ting everyone know your Crip affiliation. Now there are white teens that grew up in La Jolla, California, who can Crip Walk better than Crips from East Dago. Also, in the 1980s, if you were already past your teens and never joined a gang, you didn't become a gang mem-ber. You were lucky and missed that boat. If you lived in the suburbs you definitely didn't decide to become a gang member. In fact, an overwhelming majority of those I grew up with were poor and trying to get out of the ghetto and away from the violence. So it was and is baffling to us who lived that life that someone who had an option not to be subjected to gang life would willingly choose it. I know the glamorization of gang life through the late 1980s West Coast rap scene made the lifestyle seem appealing. For us who actually grew up in the sometimes ruthlessness of gangbanging and had no choice where we lived, there ain't nothing glamorous about watching your friends die or about attending multiple funerals annually as though it is the inevitability of one's life. That's the way it was. And for many, it's that way until you die. And it was that way for me while I was growing up in Southeast San Diego. And that lifestyle was at its peak when I came to East Dago.

Once I became laser-focused on becoming a member of the East Dago Mob, I pledged my allegiance to it and to the money making, even if it meant death or life in prison. As I said earlier, I repeated the mantra, "I'd rather live a short rich life than a long poor life," and like many who represented East Dago Mob during that time, we took those words to heart and lived our lives accordingly. In fact for some of us death couldn't have been too much worse than where and how we were living.

It's common to hear stories about young people being "jumped in" as an initiation into a gang. Getting jumped in usually consisted of several gang members attacking the prospective gang member until the gang has determined the prospect has heart and can fight. It's usually just a test to see if you are committed enough to join the gang. I've seen it happen myself on a number of occasions, but that's not what happened to Dave and me when we joined the East Dago Mob. Dave and I had decided early on that we were going to be ambitious as gang members and drug dealers, and we knew even though we were new to the area we were going to become members of the East Dago Mob.

As I said, East Dago Mob was different from a lot of the gangs in Southeast. One main difference was that just because you lived in the neighborhood didn't mean you could claim you were from East Dago Mob. Additionally East Dago Mob was more organized than the average street gang, because of its small size, and it could for the most part actually monitor who was and wasn't a member, unlike some of the larger gangs in Southeast.

For all intents and purposes, Dave and I decided after living in East Dago for a while, we were just going to join the Mob. Of course this got back to some of the OGs who were shot callers, and they didn't appreciate our decision that we were going to become members without going through the proper protocol such as getting jumped in or getting the ok from an OG. I know if we had grown up in the area we would have had an easier time becoming members, but most of the shot callers didn't know us, although we had been in the neighborhood for over a year and hanging out with many of the lower ranked East Dago Mob members.

During this time East Dago Mob was a different beast from most gangs. It was more of a privilege than a right to call oneself a member. We were confronted multiple times about assuming we could just claim the neighborhood without going through the proper channels and initiations. Dave and I, though we cared, knew who we were and what we could bring to the neighborhood as we had experienced gang wars and drug dealers firsthand in the heart of Southeast. The drug dealing and killing wasn't new to us, and we were ambitious and eager to make a name for ourselves. That is exactly what would happen even before we became official members of the East Dago Mob.

As Dave and I sold our drugs on 44th Street and hung out with other 44th Street Hustlers or 44 Blocc Hustlers, which was a clique within the East Dago Mob, we began to earn our reputation not necessarily as tough guys or gangsters, but as two youngsters who were down and ready to prove ourselves. We were hustlers and wouldn't hesitate to let everyone know it. You also had the Lil Neighborhood or Lil Naybors from East Dago Mob which was another subset. However, back then there was really no distinction when it came to representing East Dago. We were one.

My first unofficial initiation into the East Dago Mob occurred after a verbal confrontation Dave had one night at Highland Park with another East Dago Mob member named Bullock. This would ultimately escalate into my own physical confrontation with a shot caller named Lunnie Dunnie that same night, and then lead to Dave and my first real test as new members of the Mob since we first arrived on the block some months prior.

Bullock was only a year or two older than Dave and me and was already a reputable East Dago Mob member. The funny thing is that it had been Dave and Bullock exchanging words, and I was just standing there, but because Dave and I were best friends and damn near conjoined twins because we were together all the time, obviously if Dave got into it with someone, I did too, and vice versa. That's just how it was with us when we moved to East Dago.

I vaguely recall what Dave and Bullock were arguing about, but it had something to do with Dave calling Bullock a nigga during casual conversation and Bullock took offense to it. I never really understood why Bullock took offense to it because that was a word we all used dozens of times a day referring to each other. It was a word of endearment and at the time Bullock wasn't a Black Power kind of guy who despised the word nigga. Obviously there was something else going on, and Dave calling Bullock a nigga was Bullock's opening to go at him. About thirty minutes after the argument ended Dave went home for the night.

I lived right across the street and was still hanging out at Highland

Park. About thirty or so minutes later out of nowhere Lunnie Dunnie and two other guys, along with Bullock, came walking towards the park as I was sitting on a bench. Bullock pointed me out and told Lunnie Dunnie, "That's one of them right there." Lunnie Dunnie began grabbing on me, asking me about what happened earlier with Dave and Bullock. This definitely caught me off guard, because from my vantage point and understanding, I thought it was just an innocuous argument between two niggas from the same neighborhood and never thought it would be more than that. Also I was just standing there and never said anything during the argument. I think maybe Bullock was expecting to see Dave still out there, but since he wasn't and I was, that was just as good.

Even though Dave and I considered ourselves official members of the East Dago Mob, most of the higher ups didn't, especially people like Lunnie Dunnie who had been around East Dago Mob since its inception. I guess Lunnie Dunnie and Bullock may have felt Dave and I were still relatively new to the neighborhood and had no right to challenge them in any way. In a way I guess East Dago Mob in those days was like the Italian mafia, where if you're not a made member and you're only an associate, you don't have certain privileges. I get it now.

Lunnie Dunnie was a huge dude standing over six feet and weighing at least twice what I did. I'm not going to lie and try to sound like I was a tough guy. I was intimidated as hell, but not scared. I was like "Fuck it; if I get beat down, oh well, I'll just deal with it whatever that is." At any rate, I ended up just getting grabbed and roughed up a little and then they left. Although there were a lot of other people out there in the park at the time, they were either neutral or had more loyalty to Bullock and Lunnie Dunnie and weren't going to come to my aid. I was by myself and had no weapon on me, but I stood there and never tried to leave during the entire altercation. Right after the incident my sister and mother tried to make me go inside our apartment, but there was no way I was going to show any fear and go inside. I stayed outside, stayed in Highland Park, and posted up for a few more hours.

I had already made the determination that what happened to me that night would never happen again. There's no question Lunnie Dunnie was a shot caller from East Dago Mob and was dangerous, but I too was becoming a rida in my own right, which meant I was expected to a formidable active gang member and experience the fighting and shooting up close and personal in furtherance of my gang. Taking an ass whooping by one of my homies, if it was necessary, was nothing. Homies in the hood fight all the time, and usually you shake hands afterwards and drink a forty-ounce or smoke a joint together. However, this was different. There was some personal animosity toward Dave and me, and it had nothing to do with the usual hood type of stuff. Furthermore, I was beyond that short skinny kid who got my ass whooped for nothing. That just wasn't me. I had a front seat to the wars on the Four Corners of Death, and my mentality was I'd rather die or go to the California Youth Authority than be a bitch. So after Lunnie Dunnie rushed me at the park that night, I knew that would change me forever as a gang member.

I think everyone who was present that night or who heard about what happened just figured I would be scared and stay away for a while, but I knew if I was ever going to earn respect to become an official East Dago Mobsta, I had to post-up, which meant hanging out on the front line to show we had heart no matter the potential consequences. Once Dave found out what happened to me the night before at Highland Park, we vowed that we would be prepared if something like that ever happened again.

The following day Dave and I paid a guy who was a smoker (one of our regular crack cocaine customers) in crack cocaine to purchase an M-1 rifle and a twelve-gauge shotgun from Kmart. Back then if you were over twenty-one years old and had a valid ID, you could go into Kmart and purchase a rifle or shotgun without any waiting period or background check. You could leave with the weapon the same day. We gave the smoker the cash to make the gun purchases and after the smoker gave us the guns, Dave and I immediately went to the hardware store on 40th Street and University Avenue and purchased a hacksaw. Once we got back to my apartment, we sawed off both the rifle and shotgun so they could be easily concealed.

In the days that followed my Kmart gun purchase, I hadn't given what happened with me and Lunnie Dunnie too much thought. However, I was apprehensive because he had a serious reputation and I knew I would have to see him again. Over the next two or three nights Dave and I would post up on 44th Street in front of my apartments or hang out at Highland Park like always. We would keep the guns hidden in a utility box on the side of the apartment complex so we could grab them as quickly as possible in case we needed them. During this time the potential for a confrontation with crosstown enemies was immense and the guns were not solely for the purpose of my anxiety over Lunnie Dunnie.

Although I wasn't physically hurt from my confrontation with Lunnie Dunnie, I knew that there was a serious possibility that he would approach me again. Dave and I had straightened out our differences with Bullock, but we heard rumors that Lunnie Dunnie didn't like us and had an issue with me in particular. At the same time, Dave and I didn't want any major beef with anyone from East Dago. Nonetheless, we weren't going to be punks. Furthermore, considering Lunnie Dunnie's massive size, I didn't think Dave or I could take him one-on-one. Not only was Lunnie Dunnie huge, he was known to be good with his hands as well. And at that point I don't think fighting was even considered.

Dave was barely sixteen years old and I was approaching seventeen, and we were both no taller than five feet six inches and maybe weighing 160 pounds drenched in water with clothes on. We knew that if we used those guns we purchased and harmed anyone, we would face serious time in the California Youth Authority. We also knew that we weren't the only ones with guns and Lunnie Dunnie in particular had access to guns and would likely not hesitate to use them.

Now I don't want to send the message that it was okay for Dave and me to contemplate harming someone with a firearm, nor do I want it to seem like I was a coward who was afraid to fight and had to resort to using a weapon to defend myself. In fact, I grew up fighting, winning some and losing more. I may not have been the best fighter, but I would use my hands when necessary. However, when you're from the streets and growing up in a serious gang and drug environment and all you've seen is violence and you're dealing with people who are not necessarily bringing fists to a gun fight, you tend not to underestimate any situation. From my experience people from the hood who were quick to call other gangsters cowards for being quick with a gun were usually the ones who never had the heart to shoot, even in the direst situations.

It wasn't like Dave and I wanted to harm anyone, we could have easily been shot and killed ourselves, and that was the point. We weren't official members of East Dago Mob and there was no gang code protecting us. Furthermore, I already had gotten roughed up once for absolutely nothing, and that just wasn't about to happen again. I've had my ass whooped many times while growing up in the hood, but there's a difference between losing a fight and accepting a loss and then moving on versus going up against some potential gangsta shit. I wasn't in the mood to accept a beat down for the sake of someone's ego. I felt I earned that right on Ocean View and the Four Corners.

About three or four days went by after we purchased the M-1 and shotgun before we ran into Lunnie Dunnie again. We were standing in front of my apartment complex on 44th Street across from Highland Park when Lunnie Dunnie drove up. I had the sawed-off M-1 rifle tucked in my pants and Dave had the sawed-off double-barrel shotgun tucked in his pants. Dave and I both knew that although I was roughed up a little it was mostly grabbing and no punches were thrown, so it definitely wasn't serious enough for someone to lose their life over. It would be better to try to settle our differences than escalate the situation. This was especially important to Dave and me with someone like Lunnie Dunnie because we were still trying to get officially "put on" with the East Dago Mob, and having Lunnie Dunnie vouch for us would be a good start.

Within a couple of minutes we decided to plan our approach to the situation as Lunnie Dunnie pulled up on the block and stood in front of the apartments talking to some other guys from the neighborhood. Dave told me that I should just stay back near the stairs, which were about halfway in my apartment complex. Since Lunnie Dunnie for some reason had an issue with me and not so much with Dave, Dave said he would go up there and talk to him and I should stay back. Dave and I both knew that my presence might escalate the situation unnecessarily. I could still see and somewhat hear everything that was being said. Even though I really didn't want any drama there was tension between us, and Dave and I still had to walk that neighborhood. We weren't going to stay in the house, so we knew that eventually it was going to have to be resolved one way or another and tonight would be that night.

Unfortunately when you factor in tension between Lunnie Dunnie and me and the easy accessibility of weapons and alcohol, things could get out of control really fast. I wasn't afraid but I knew it was smart that Dave told me to stay back while he tried to resolve the matter. To see and hear Dave and Lunnie Dunnie talk in a civil manner was somewhat of a relief, but I was prepared for whatever the outcome.

DON'T LET YOUR PAST HOLD YOU BACK

After Dave and Lunnie Dunnie talked, our issues with Lunnie Dunnie were resolved. We didn't suddenly become buddies or anything overnight, though in the months that followed we would become close homies. However, the tension was dissipated and we could move forward.

Until now besides Dave and me, no one actually knew about the behind-the-scenes details of that situation with Lunnie Dunnie. Dave and I never spoke of it, and like other memories, this is the first time I'm bringing it to light as I tell the story in this book. It definitely wasn't something we wanted to brag about back then. It was just one of those things that happened in the hood.

Everyone in the neighborhood had a nickname or a gang moniker. I was known as LB for my middle and last initial, but as my reputation in the streets increased, one of my big homies, Bill "Billy Bob" Collins, started calling me Gunsmoke.* He said I reminded him of Gunsmoke because I...well I always had a lot of guns. Billy Bob said every time he saw me I had a gun and was ready for war. Gunsmoke eventually stuck, along with LB, and even today most of my homies who knew me back then still call me LB and some even call me Gunsmoke. It's kind of ironic that I was once nicknamed Gunsmoke, but today I can't stand the sight of a gun in person. I've witnessed too much pain and tragedy because of guns. Even if I weren't a felon, I would probably never own a gun again.

During this time in East Dago, and Southeast San Diego, where we would also travel through several times a day, any little encounter with someone could escalate into something deadly, even if the intention was just to fight. Sometimes when I hear people say, "Why can't we go back to the days when we only used our fists?" honestly I don't remember those days after I was thirteen. Sure there were a lot of fights, but there was a lot of killing going on too. And the quickest way to get killed where I grew up was to only bring fists to a gun fight.

I had seen enough gun violence firsthand prior to turning sixteen for me to get caught slippin' in the streets because I wanted to show someone I was willing to fight. If I had to fight I would, but I also got the name Gunsmoke because I didn't want to get caught parading around thinking the next guy only wanted to use his hands.

Beginning in Bakersfield when my sisters' boyfriends pulled out guns right in front of me to intimidate other gang members to my days on Ocean View Boulevard and the Four Corners of Death, witnessing or hearing about people getting stabbed or shot was a daily occurrence. Therefore, by the time I was sixteen years old and came to the block in East Dago, I had already become numb to the gun play. If fighting was an option, I was down, but I would also never bring only my fists to a gunfight. It was gangsta in those streets, and it had nothing to do with anyone being a coward. It was kill or be killed or watch your homies die.

Eventually I started hanging out with some of the higher ups within the East Dago Mob who normally didn't hang out with us at Highland Park. Although Dave and I were still relatively new and low level members in the East Dago Mob, it was no longer an issue for most, especially those who were from 44 Blocc Hustlas and hung out with us every day. We had skipped the traditional gang initiation of getting "jumped in" and proved our loyalty and heart by showing we were willing to sacrifice life and liberty for the Mob, not just a few scratches and bruises.

Of course it would take a lot more proving to earn my respect as an East Dago Mobsta, but it wouldn't take long. Anyone who was around during that era can attest; some people got jumped into the Mob, others were accepted by right of birth or because they had lived in East Dago most of their lives. Dave and I had to literally shoot our way into the Mob. We were very impressionable and ambitious at the time and would almost do anything to belong to something that was bigger than us and that gave us meaning. East Dago Mob was the thing that was in front of us and consumed our lives. Neither Dave nor I had grown up with a father in the home, nor did we have any significant positive male role models around us. Even though I am very remorseful about ever joining a gang and have serious regrets for some things I have done, I can honestly say I believe most of what I've experienced was inevitable, and I try not to be too hard on myself about some of the decisions I've made, even though I regret them. I own my past.

Earning my reputation as an East Dago Mobsta wouldn't allow for me to take a day off. It was like a full-time job and I was on call twenty-four hours a day, seven days a week. If I wasn't dedicating my days and nights to selling drugs and gangbanging, I was out hanging with my friends getting drunk and getting at girls. That was that East Dago Mob life in the 1980s.

Although I was still a small-time corner drug dealer, occasionally I would end up selling crack in one of the crack houses in the neighborhood. For rent we would give the occupants of the house or apartment crack cocaine in lieu of paying any money for rent. The people who lived there were still able to stay there as long as they didn't interfere with the residence being run as a crack house. There was no shortage of rich drug dealers in East Dago because of its location with hundreds of apartment complexes and houses available for crack cocaine selling and being away from the fierce competition in Southeast in the mid to late 1980s.

If you had any ability to be a hustler and were smart, you had a chance at rising as a high-level drug dealer in East Dago. However, I had been selling crack for about a year or so, but for some reason I could not make the leap from petty drug dealer to baller status. I had the ambition since my days on the Four Corners of Death. I had been associating daily with some of the ballers and had even worked for several of them, but after selling all of my drugs and receiving my cut, I would only have several hundred dollars left over, which I would usually spend on food, clothes, and alcohol. I look back on this time and understand my rationale for spending everything I had and not saving. I had grown up going without enough food to eat at times, and if I did have enough to eat, it would usually be leftover pinto beans for breakfast, lunch, and dinner for a number of days, so whenever I had money in my pocket, I spent it on whatever type of food I liked. Clothes were my next favorite item to purchase. I had been ridiculed since the sixth grade because of my clothes and shoes. Rarely did I ever have a chance to wear any name brands before I started selling drugs.

Even though I aspired to be one of the richest drug dealers in my city, I was not saving or investing my money.

Although I had immersed myself in gangbanging, which took up a significant amount of time and energy, money had always been a priority of mine. I had become increasingly frustrated about my continued status as a low-level drug dealer. I would see ballers every day, and some of them were in my circle of homies and acquaintances, but I felt like I was not coming up fast enough and was still a small-time drug dealer. I would have money in my hands and count out thousands of dollars, but at the end of the day I turned most of it over to my boss and was left with maybe five or six hundred dollars, which wasn't too bad for a seventeen-year-old living in the hood. However, I longed to learn the secret to getting rich, street rich that is. Was there some complicated formula or laundry list of do's and don'ts? Was there some ancient Chinese secret to getting big money as a drug dealer?

For almost two years, including going back to my days working with EJ, I held thousands of dollars in my hand, but hardly any of it was mine. Having the right connection, or lack thereof in my case, played a major role, but I was already rubbing the right elbows in the game but continued to have a poor man's mentality, and the amount of money I had stacked that was mine showed it. Nonetheless I would continue to watch closely and pick the brains of those who were successful drug dealers and had a lot of money, and the secret to my problem of not coming up in the game would eventually be revealed.

Probably one of the most important lessons I had to learn in order to increase my status in the dope game was I needed to start saving my money. Instead of saving I had been spending all my profit on bullshit like one-hundred-plus dollar Air Jordan tennis shoes and three-hundred-dollar Fila sweat suits, just to name a few meaningless material items that a small time drug dealer had no business purchasing.

I had been wasting my money on meaningless material things before I could afford them. Instead of reinvesting, or as we called it, "re-upping," all my money and putting away the profit in savings, I was spending everything I had, whether it was my cut from working for someone or from selling my own drugs. Basically I had to learn to save and invest.

As crazy as it might sound, what I was learning in the drug business would also help me later in life. Just like many others who were trying to become successful in whatever profession they chose, I had to have the mindset of delayed gratification, which is an invaluable trait to have in any walk of life or profession, whether it's education or climbing the corporate ladder. I think what I learned most around this time was there are no shortcuts to success—at least not for most people, and that included people in the dope game. That same lesson would be revisited many years later when I decided to get my life in order and take the long arduous journey to become a lawyer.

However, during this period of my life I was focused on becoming a crack cocaine kingpin. Once I actually implemented my own daily hustle, I started to see myself being catapulted in the direction that had been elusive for me over the prior couple of years. In a very short time I went from having only several hundred dollars of profit to a few thousand dollars saved up. I still didn't have the connections or enough money to purchase any significant amount of drugs to turn a larger profit and really start balling, but as long as I stayed on the path, I knew someone would eventually take me under his wing and bring me in as a full partner or turn me on to his connection.

I had no free passes in those East Dago streets. I didn't grow up in East Dago, nor was I around in the early PBI days besides my brief time attending Wilson and Horace Mann Junior High Schools in the seventh grade. I knew that to get the respect I would have to handle my business when it came to gangbanging, even if it meant dying young or going to prison for the rest of my life. And as horrible and sad as it might sound, back in those days most of the guys I hung around didn't care about dying or going to prison for life. Certainly none of us wanted to die or go to prison, but it was like a rite-of-passage, and we all understood it and embraced it as a way of life for us. Unless you are a black or brown male growing up in the streets of Southern California, you might never understand that mentality. Even today with all the places I have been fortunate enough to see, all of my travels around the country and abroad, my educational, professional, and financial success, I still understand the mind of a gangbanger because I was one, a real one.

I never took for granted that I was involved in a very deadly business of drug dealing and gangbanging. I had grown up watching people I knew get murdered for this street bullshit. I was aware that every time I walked outside my mother's apartment there was only a 50 percent chance I would make it home that night. Although I had become laser focused on having money, I always took the violence around me serious and never underestimated someone else's gangsta.

My status as a drug dealer had been increasing but I never forgot what

I was up against in the streets and what I had been through dodging bullets and death on a daily. In fact even though I was beginning to be around a lot of so-called high rollers, it was hard for me to respect a drug dealer just because he had money. A lot of ballers instigated gang or other street politics and when the shit hit the fan and it was time for war, they expected their little homies, or the ridas, as we called those who put it all on the line, to put in the work and risk their lives or freedom. Gangbanging is a deadly way of life, with all of its ignorance and genocide. If you chose to live that life you'd better live up to what you claimed, because you'd best believe your enemy did.

Even though I was selling drugs on a daily basis and making some decent money, I still lived at home with my mother, though this wasn't unusual for a youngest child who was a mama's boy. Furthermore, I was only seventeen years old and technically still a minor, even though I was acting like, or at least thought I was already, an adult.

I had never lived apart from my mother except for several very brief periods when she had to go to Oakland to look after my grandmother and when I briefly stayed with my father after he moved back to San Diego from Florida. It had always been me and my mother even going back to when I was seven years old and right after the divorce, with my sisters coming in and out ocassionally. I knew sooner or later I would have to leave the nest but wasn't expecting it to occur so abruptly.

CHAPTER 7

I Shot The Sheriff

AROUND LATE 1987 or early 1988 I had rekindled a relationship with my junior high school sweetheart Cynthia. I don't remember how Cynthia and I started dating again, but she had grown up in East Dago and was an original member of Playgirls Incorporated (PGI), the female version of PBI. She started coming around after I became an East Dago Mob member. She would come over and visit with me at the apartment I now shared with my mother and her boyfriend Denver. He and my mother had been dating off and on since I was thirteen, and they too, like Cynthia and me, had recently gotten back together.

Cynthia was a year older than me and had already finished high school and was working. She still lived at home with her mother in a different part of town but had begun spending most of her time at my place. Over the months she and I had discussed getting our own place together. She had a job and I was selling a lot of drugs at the time, but I was still comfortable living at home with my mother, even though I didn't particularly like Denver. However, an incident would soon force me to make the decision to finally leave the nest and move out on my own with Cynthia.

Denver was a humongous man. He wasn't very tall, but I was probably only five feet six inches tall by now and all but one hundred and fifty pounds. Denver's six-foot-something height and two hundred fifty plus pounds made me look like a shrimp. I had known Denver since I was thirteen and he and I always got along well but not so much when I got older. The difference between when he and my mother were first dating and now was Denver didn't live with us back then and he didn't have a serious drinking and drug problem—at least not that I knew of.

I was aware of the fact that Denver used crack cocaine, but he didn't use it to the point that he would steal anything out of my mother's apartment to support his habit, at least not that I was aware of. And although I vehemently disapproved of him smoking crack because he was living in our apartment and he was my mother's boyfriend, he was relatively normal to me when I knew he was on crack. However, when Denver drank alcohol, it was a totally different story.

Although Denver never committed any domestic violence against my mother, he became extremely belligerent every time he got drunk. I think because he knew that he was much bigger than everyone in the house and pretty much bigger than everyone else outside, he acted like a bully. However, he was an overall nice guy until he became drunk and that was probably the only reason I put up with him for so long. I wasn't afraid of him, but I was intimidated by him when he got drunk. Of course I would never allow him or anyone else ever to put their hands on my mother, but when Denver started drinking heavily he would walk around the apartment as if he were the king, and if anyone challenged him in any way, he cut them down with his belligerence.

Although Denver's drunken tirades didn't happen very often, they happened enough that it really started to affect me in ways it hadn't before. I grew up protecting my mother and sisters from men because I was the only male at home, so there would be no hesitation to do what I had to do if Denver ever crossed a line to violence. But even though Denver had never put his hands on anyone in the home, he would threaten us repeatedly, and by his mere size had everyone walking on eggshells when he was drunk.

I was becoming aware that one of the main reasons I thought about moving out was that I was becoming a man and a very active gang member and drug dealer, and it was only a matter of time before Denver's and my personality would clash. I still respected him because he was an adult and he was my mother's boyfriend, but there was only so much a person in my position could take. I was literally in life-or-death situations every day surrounded by killers; there was no way I was going to take bullying in my own home for much longer.

One night while Cynthia and I were sitting on the living room couch watching television and talking in my mother's apartment, Denver was going on one of his drunken tirades and walking around the apartment cussing at everyone for no apparent reason other than showing he was King Kong. As much as I wanted to try to ignore him like usual, something was different about this day and may have been brewing for a while.

I was seventeen years old and coming into my own and had little tolerance for any man challenging me, especially when my mother, sisters, or girlfriend were involved. Also, I must have been having a bad day or something, but on this night I was just fed up with Denver. He kept walking in and out of the living room cursing and giving Cynthia and me dirty looks. He then stopped and looked right at Cynthia and called her a bitch. I don't know what caused him to call her a bitch, but I snapped and he and I started arguing. It was one thing for him to disrespect me; I was used to it. It was a whole other thing, for no good reason, to call my girlfriend a bitch. She hadn't said or done anything to him.

DON'T LET YOUR PAST HOLD YOU BACK

After Denver and I argued for about forty seconds, I smiled and told Cynthia I would be right back. I didn't have a gun with me so I went to my homie Melle Mel's who lived only a few blocks away. I knew he would hand me a pistol with no hesitation and not ask any questions. I wasn't certain that I was going to come back and shoot Denver, but I knew he had crossed a line. I also knew there was no way I was going to allow Denver to physically harm me or my girlfriend or mother, so I had thoughts of doing what I felt I needed to do.

Denver knew I was furious when I left the apartment, and he still continued to be belligerent as I was walking down the stairs. I doubt he realized what I was intending to get. If he had, he was stupid to stay there. I probably thought I would just leave for a while to cool off and give him a chance to sober up like I had done many times before. I admit I never really thought he would hit my mother, but I just didn't know, from his intoxicated behavior. Usually I would just leave for a while and when I returned it was all good and things would be back to normal; well, normal in my world, anyway.

However, this night would be different. I didn't know for sure if Denver would approach me when I returned. To be honest things could have turned out peacefully like it had before, but this time there was no turning back.

After getting the gun from Melle Mel I returned to my mother's apartment. I must have had a look of rage in my eyes, because DJL, who was standing in front of the apartments hustling, jumped in front of me and tried to stop me from going upstairs. All I can remember is having the gun out and saying something to the effect that "I'm about to smoke this fool." DJL's effort to stop me was futile, as I continued my pursuit toward the stairs. DJL likely knew I was about to do something awful within a couple of minutes or less and his night of hustling on 44 would be over, and my life, at least as someone free, would likely be over as well.

As I started walking up the stairs to my mother's apartment, Denver came out of the doorway and stood at the top of the stairs with my sister Rhonda, who also lived upstairs right next door to us. I was about halfway up the stairs staring at Denver as he stared down at me. I can honestly say that if Denver had been calm at that moment and tried to deescalate the situation, I would not have done what I did next.

I don't think Denver had any idea of what was going through my mind and that he finally had pushed me to the point that I wanted to end his life or at least seriously injure him. As I got closer to the top of the stairs, I didn't say a word but knew if he said one thing to me that was disrespectful I was going to shoot him. He began talking shit to me as I approached him. He started cussing me out again, and before he could utter any more words, I pointed the gun directly at his upper torso and pulled the trigger.

I can regretfully but honestly say I was hoping to kill him at that point. When I pointed the gun at him, however, it gave him enough time to react. This six-foot-something, two-hundred-pound-plus man moved like he was a track star with acrobatic skills. He turned right when I pulled the trigger and ran back into the apartment.

I knew I had shot Denver because I was only a few feet away when I pulled the trigger aiming directly at him. It was dark and I had never been to a gun range, but I knew I couldn't be that bad of a shot, no matter how fast he reacted. I waited a few seconds for Cynthia to come out of the apartment. She ran down the stairs then we jumped in my car and left. I drove straight to Dave's house for the night.

Although I knew I had shot Denver, I didn't stay around to find out how he was doing. It didn't take long for me to get pages on my beeper and start hearing the details about Denver's condition. God was with Denver and me that night because I tried to kill him and didn't. I had had enough of his bullying. I pointed the gun directly at him with every intention of inflicting the most harm I could, but thanks to his quick reaction by running back into the apartment, the bullet only grazed him.

Denver dodged a bullet literally and figuratively. I did too, because if I had inflicted any serious harm on Denver that night, my life would likely be dramatically different today. I likely would have been sent to the California Youth Authority until I was twenty-five years old, and I was seventeen at the time. Eight years of my youth would have been spent behind bars, time wasted because of my temper and an idiot who pushed me to my limit. Denver was an asshole when he got drunk, but he didn't deserve to die for it, and I thank God to this day he didn't.

Even though the bullet had only grazed Denver, the ambulance came and took him to the hospital. Someone told me that as the paramedics were loading Denver into the ambulance, the police questioned him about who shot him and he told them that it was me. Yeah Denver snitched on me. One of the gang detectives present after the shooting left my mother a business card for me to give him a call. I think I laughed the following day when my mother tried to give me the business card. I thought to myself, sure I'll call him, yeah right.

Denver was released from the hospital the same night and came back to my mother's apartment. I'm assuming he was either still drunk, got drunk again, or maybe crazier than me, because when he got home from the hospital he broke out the windshield of my second car I left parked outside the apartment complex. Damn! What a stupid mothafucka. I JUST TRIED TO KILL HIM! I thought Denver must have been crazy or stupid, or both.

When I came back to my mother's apartment the following morning and saw my windshield broken, initially I was angry for about a minute. It's like he didn't realize I could have easily gone right upstairs and finished what I had intended to do the night before, but I wasn't even angry as I was when I shot him. I just took a deep breath and then I had to laugh to myself. I thought for a second, I just shot this nigga; at least I could give him that. So what if he broke a windshield? I would have it fixed by the end of the day and I did. The next day I had to laugh again.

No charges were ever brought against me for shooting Denver, and I doubt the police or Denver ever pressed the issue. Believe it or not by that next day I was no longer angry at Denver. I knew, however, I had to move out and would never sleep at my mother's apartment again as long as Denver was living there.

When things finally settled down and got back to normal, my mother and I finally had a chance to talk about what had occurred. We agreed it was time for me to move. I never gave my mother an ultimatum that it was either Denver or me, nor did she tell me I had to leave, but I knew after what happened I could no longer live there. I was a young man already living my life, and living a very violent and dangerous one at that. It was time for me to move on.

Cynthia and I stayed at hotels and when Cynthia went home, I stayed with Dave until she and I eventually found our own apartment. Oddly, after the night of the shooting and I moved out, Denver and I actually became closer than we had ever been. In hindsight, the scene kind of reminds me of the movie *Baby Boy*,* but this happened to me almost thirty years before that movie was even written. In *Baby Boy*, the mother found a new boyfriend who the son hated and ended up having a violent confrontation with. At the end of the movie, the son finally leaves the nest and he and his mother's boyfriend become friends.

I believe God has a strange way of showing us things. I had known for a while I needed to move out and be on my own, but it took something that could have turned out very tragic to force me to make the leap. I regret what happened to Denver that night. He wasn't a bad person. I own my past.

CHAPTER 8

Too Close to Home

IN 1988 MY life had been about gangbanging and selling crack with everything else finding its way in between. One night, my homie Baby T, who was an East Dago Mob affiliate and an original Ghost Town Crip member, along with Lunnie Dunnie, and my good friend Lil Crazy who was from West Coast Rollin 30s Crips, were all hanging out at Baby T's and my spot where we lived and also sold drugs.

Business was somewhat slow on this particular night and we were just sitting around basing on each other. Basing was when family members or friends sat around and bagged on each other, commonly known as "playing the dozens." We were doing what homies do, laughing, drinking, and just having a good time.

After about an hour of us just chilling, Lil Crazy and Lunnie Dunnie decided to leave at the same time, although they didn't come together. I was sitting on the couch in the living room watching television while Baby T sat at the dining room table counting money and drugs. Within a couple of minutes after Lil Crazy and Lunnie Dunnie left my apartment, I heard a loud pop. It was the sound of a gunshot. Baby T and I both knew instantly what that sound was, and our instincts immediately kicked in. We both simultaneously ran and grabbed our guns and went outside to see what happened. Our spot was on the second floor, and as soon as we got to the stairs and looked down on the ground floor, we could see Lunnie Dunnie holding Lil Crazy in his arms and crying.

By the time Baby T and I got downstairs, Lunnie Dunnie just kept repeating while he was weeping, "I didn't mean to do it." A neighbor came outside and tried to resuscitate Lil Crazy, but to no avail. Lunnie Dunnie had shot Lil Crazy in the head with a nine millimeter pistol. As if it happened yesterday, I will never forget Lil Crazy's face as he lay on the ground. He had always had a big smile on his face. Rarely did I see Lil Crazy not smiling. As he lay, with no pulse after taking a bullet to the head, he had his big trademark Lil Crazy smile on his face.

Lunnie Dunnie said he accidentally shot Lil Crazy while he was play-ing with a gun. He said he had put the gun to Lil Crazy's head in a playful way, pretending he would shoot him, when the gun suddenly went off. Oddly enough Lunnie Dunnie's story was believable for me for a number of reasons. First, Lil Crazy and he were just upstairs for at least an hour joking and having a good time with no animosity. Also, with the unlimited number of guns we had, it was not unusual for us to play around with them occasionally, albeit knowing the dan-gers. In fact, because we had so many guns and had been in so many gun fights and seen so much violence, we were somewhat numb to the perils of guns. Moreover, I had once accidentally shot myself in the thigh with a feather-trigger gun I had in my waist while I was play fighting with Dave. I also once accidentally shot my little homie Baby Ant, Bullock's little brother. Thank God the gun was pointed down and the buckshots only ricocheted off the floor or he would be gone. So Lunnie Dunnie's explanation wasn't unbelievable for me in par-ticular, considering our lifestyle and recklessness with guns.

This is one story that's difficult for me to discuss. I remember the de-tails of my good friend losing his life in such a violent way minutes after we had been hanging out together. It happened almost thirty years ago, but recalling it feels like it just happened today. What happened that night in 1988 was one of most dramatic events that I've ever experienced, and even though it still hurts thinking about it, I feel compelled to share.

After everything settled down the night of Lil Crazy's death and all the authorities finished their investigation and took Lunnie Dunnie away to jail for murder, Baby T and I went back upstairs and told each other we were done with guns forever. We knew people who had been shot and some even murdered. We also had witnessed or been around shootings going back to our early teens, but this was different. It was too close to home, and this one had really done something to our psyche. We had all just been hanging out together. Lil Crazy was our loved one, and to add insult to injury, he was taken away, albeit by accident, by one of our own.

That night, Baby T and I put all our guns away and swore we were done with the weapons and violence. However, our anti-gun stance would last about only a day or so, and then we came back to reality. The guns we put up that night and swore we'll never hold again were back out and we were back to street life as usual.

Rest in Paradise, Tim, aka Lil Crazy, aka Lil Crazy Mike.

CHAPTER 9

Aspirations of a Drug Kingpin

I WAS NO longer living on 44th Street, but I was still hustling there and hanging out there just about every day.

"What's up, fool? How much money do you have saved?"

"I have about five thousand dollars" was my response to Fat Steve, aka Fat Daddy, as I leaned over through the window of his custom black Cadillac. Fat Steve was a member of East Dago Mob. East Dago didn't have any formal ranking system, but if it did, I would put Fat Steve in the category of a lieutenant or captain, someone who had status as a major hustler and/or had a reputation as a violent hitter in the streets. The captains were either the main hitters and/or money makers who associated closely with the generals who were the top ballers and shot callers of the East Dago Mob. I would have been considered a frontline soldier and rising lieutenant, whether selling drugs on the street corner or in a crack house, always on the frontlines ready for war.

Although most of the lieutenants and captains were on the frontlines at times, they had the status and money that gave them a higher ranking in the Mob. Even a few generals from East Dago Mob, such as Big Boo Gist, Henry "Hen Dog" Farve, Eric "EC" Collins, and Big Charlie

Steele aka Big CS, would still post up with young frontline soldiers like myself and even put in work in the streets if necessary.

Fat Steve was definitely a reputable East Dago Mob member. Unlike me, Fat Steve had grown up in East Dago, but his reputation was earned not given to him by right of birth, or because he grew up in the neighborhood. He had been a formidable Crip in the mid-1980s before he started hustling, and now he had money, baller status, and connections.

"Get in the car, little homie," Fat Steve told me. Unlike some of the older homies with money and who were shot callers from East Dago Mob, that didn't stop Fat Steve from hanging out with the younger homies and less successful hustlers. He would still post up with us on 44th Street and at Highland Park as well as other places, especially when we left East Dago in a large group and caravanned to Southeast.

Fat Steve knew firsthand not only the young homies on the block's ambition as drug dealers, but our willingness to do whatever to enforce our territory and prove ourselves to the high-ups in the Mob. I also knew Fat Steve had connections to help me get to the next level.

Once I was in the car with Fat Steve, he asked me if I wanted to go half with him. This meant I had a chance to purchase a large quantity of cocaine and be his business partner. Fat Steve continued to talk while I was sitting in the passenger seat of his car. While he was driving from 44th Street to the Lil Neighborhood another meet-up destination for members of East Dago Mob about six or seven blocks away, I was thinking, *LB you are on your way*. I knew this was finally an opportunity for me to come up, and I was going to take advantage of it.

I was already determined to get rich or die trying, twenty-five years before rapper 50 Cent marketed the term. From my days on the Four

Corners, I had resigned myself to getting rich, getting murdered, going to prison, or all three in pursuit of my ghetto dreams. I didn't visualize any other life for myself by the time I turned sixteen. Poor most of my life and dealing with the harsh realities of the inner city, I didn't see any other way to get a piece of the American Dream. Although I cared about the risks related to achieving my objectives, however, I believed the potential gain outweighed the risks.

I had been struggling as an off-and-on street-corner drug dealer for a couple of years, and I finally became what we called in my neighborhood "ghetto rich." Since Fat Steve and I were business partners now, he vouched for me and eventually introduced me to one of his connections, L.A. Jeff, who was a baller out of Los Angeles.

Fat Steve and I eventually opened a crack house in the Lil Neighborhood and were able to sell large quantities of crack cocaine out of it for several months. We also sold semi-quantities of weight or wholesale amounts of crack cocaine to other drug dealers throughout the city.

I estimate that Fat Steve and I were making roughly ten thousand dollars a week in our crack house alone, and that didn't include the weight we were selling wholesale to other drug dealers. That wasn't small change for an eighteen and nineteen year old. Fat Steve and I we were making so much money so fast that it wasn't unusual for us to sell out of drugs, and before we would re-up and purchase new drugs at wholesale value, we would allow other members of East Dago Mob to sell their drugs out of our crack house. We usually took a day off and hoped that when we were ready our supplier had what we needed to purchase for resale.

Our luck, however, finally ran out when we got raided by the Yellow Jackets, the San Diego Police Department's narcotics task force. We called them Yellow Jackets because every one of the police officers involved in the raid wore a yellow jacket with Police or San Diego Narcotics written on the back of it.

Because of my earlier years in Southeast and all of the people I knew from that side of town, I had dozens of people from different areas and various gangs coming to East Dago to purchase drugs from me. Some of these people were traditional rivals to East Dago, and occasionally issues arose, but not too often. I was selling wholesale amounts to others who were also buying from me to resell, so we always tried to keep it business and there was rarely, with a few exceptions, any set tripping—gang affiliation issues. For East Dago Mob, business transactions trumped gangbanging. There were always enough hours in the day for gangbanging. Plus I already had enough gang conflicts going on to not allow it to interject into my lucrative drug business.

At the age of eighteen during my peak in the drug game, I purchased two BMWs; had a custom classic 1963 convertible Chevy Impala, a townhouse, and a safe full of money; and was a silent partner in a used-car dealership. I was running in circles with major drug dealers from around San Diego and Los Angeles. Not only was I making a name for myself as a drug dealer, but also the various gang wars that erupted also allowed me to earn a formidable reputation as a member of the East Dago Mob. But even with all of the money I was making and my concerted effort to stay focused on hustling, my gang association and the reputation I acquired kept me entangled in gang violence.

My life was filled with dangers. And it was exciting at times. There was never a dull moment in my life after I turned sixteen, and it kept my adrenaline flowing. I was always in fear of going to jail, getting robbed, or getting murdered, but I knew those things came with the job description of drug dealer and gang member and I accepted the consequences. I own my past.

CHAPTER 10

Playing Tag with Satan

MY LIFESTYLE WAS always filled with excitement and trepidation. After I got chased by the police at Highland Park or got into shootouts on 44th Street, my sister Rhonda would always say, "Lamontt, don't make me and Mama have to bury you." Although I cared about whether I lived or died, even death felt like a rite-of-passage. I remember nights hanging out at Highland Park and my homie Lil Marcus and I would discuss if we got murdered how we wanted to die. We felt like dying young in the streets was inevitable anyway, so if we had to go, why not go out how we wanted to, albeit in a violent way? That way of thinking is distorted and sad, but for us back then it was normal. When I look back on that time and how I used to think, I'm amazed at how far I've come in the way I perceive the world now and life in general. Lil Marcus' perception of the world would positively change as well, unfortunately the streets would cost him a life sentence in prison for murder.

Even though most of the higher ups in the East Dago Mob had a lot of money and didn't need to hang out on 44th Street or at Highland Park anymore, we still had that camaraderie, because we were a close-knit group, even with our younger peers. Although my mother moved, my sister Rhonda still lived with my niece Coco in the apartment building across the street on 44th. My homies and I would park our cars at the park or in front of the apartments and some of us would sell drugs and others would shoot dice and get drunk and high. Around this time I had graduated to selling minimal amounts of weight exclusively and was no longer selling small quantities out of crack houses. I would purchase a large amount of cocaine and sell large amounts to various other drug dealers. This way of selling allowed me to have a lot of free time to hang out with my friends. I would spend most of my spare time driving around town in one of my nice cars just to show off or I would be at Highland Park or at the Lil Neighborhood Park.

We were a much smaller gang at the time than other gangs in Southeast, so everyone knew everyone and knew who was doing what and whether they actually had earned their stripes. It wasn't unusual for everyone to take a day off from selling drugs and meet up on 44th Street at Highland Park or at the Lil Neighborhood Park and have a barbeque or just hang out and socialize. It would be everyone, from the oldest to the youngest, from the richest to the poorest, members of East Dago Mob would be right there on the frontlines with everyone else. No matter how much money I had I would still hang out at Highland Park regularly. In my opinion no one was too important to hang out at the park on those days.

Of course there were a few people who allowed their money to go to their head and they felt like they were better than everyone else. I have some deep regrets for some of the things others and I did while I was a gang member, one thing I do think fondly of, even to this day, was the camaraderie I had with my friends during the late 1980s. We felt compelled to be close to each other and take the necessary risks to keep it all together, even if it was contrary to any decent community.

One night I was bored and decided to hang out at Highland Park and shoot dice and get drunk with my homies. When I pulled up I noticed that a handful of my friends were standing in front of my sister's apartment on 44th Street. I did what I normally would do in that situation, and we all posted up in front of the apartments drinking, shooting dice, and some people made crack sales.

It felt like an ordinary night for me, and nothing was unusual. We all knew the risks of being out in the open on such a prominent street, considering we were not only feuding with several prominent gangs from Southeast San Diego, including but not limited to, the Emerald Hills Bloods and Lil Africa Pirus, but we were also in a war with a major Los Angeles Crip gang called the 43rd Street Gangsters or 4 Tray Gangster or Gangsta Crips, as they were commonly known as. The 4 Tray's had come to San Diego and infiltrated our territory and had become acquainted with several girls from the neighborhood who we thought were disloyal to us by supplying Los Angeles gang members with inside information about the East Dago Mob. So I always had to be on guard and prepared for any possibility when I hung out, especially on 44th Street one of our main hangouts.

Because I was the constant target of the We Can gang task force of the San Diego police department, every time they saw me, they stopped and searched me without any probable cause other than I was a known gang member and drug dealer. The first thing the police did whenever they stopped me was call me by my first name, which no one ever did except certain people in my family. "Marion, you know the routine. If you don't have any guns or drugs, we'll let you go." They knew most of the time I would likely have a gun on me. After getting arrested I would bail out of jail almost immediately and usually be out by the next day.

This would happen pretty regularly, whether I was in a car that Gang Detail was familiar with or if they saw me hanging out somewhere. There were a couple of times We Can actually broke into one of my crack cocaine apartments. They knew I was inside, but I wouldn't let them in. They had no warrant or probable cause but would come through my living room window. During those searches they would find weapons or some crack and take whoever was in the house and me to jail. However, because as with the stops in my vehicle, they never had any probable cause, the district attorney would never file charges against me. It was still a game for the We Can task force. They knew by harassing me, hoping to have a reason to arrest me, knowing the district attorney would dismiss any charges, it still was a huge inconvenience and expense for me.

Eventually the We Can gang task force would be disbanded either because the district attorney got fed up with its regular unlawfulness or because of numerous citizen complaints, or both. They were truly an unlawful law enforcement group, and if I knew back then what I know now, I would have sued the hell out of them.

Because of all the potential problems with rivals as well as my concern for We Can and other law enforcement searching me for weapons, whenever I hung out at Highland Park or at the apartments across the street, I kept my assault rifle upstairs at my sister Rhonda's apartment. If something ever happened while I was hanging out and I needed to protect myself or one of my associates, I hoped one of my associates would have a weapon readily available or I would have enough time to run upstairs to Rhonda's apartment and get mine. On this particular night, however, neither would be an option, and I will never forget how close I came to death.

I could literally hear the bullets whistle over my head. I'm sure people in war have experienced this many times. Even though I had already been in a number of shootouts, this was the first time I had ever had the unnerving experience of actually feeling the air from bullets flying over my head. Immediately after a dozen or so gunshots were fired in the direction of me and my homies from East Dago Mob, I started running upstairs to Rhonda's apartment with the hopes that I could reach my gun in time to shoot back. In hindsight it was definitely unrealistic that I would have time to make it upstairs, go inside, grab my gun, and go back outside and return fire, but that was my thought process. I thought I was invincible. Of course it didn't make sense, but I got a rush from the drama. I think a lot of us felt that way whenever we were in shootouts or in some other precarious gang-related situation.

You never really had a day off from the high until there was a funeral for one of your friends, and then sadness and regrets would come over you for at least a day or so, and then it would be back to the usual. What felt like an eternity had likely only been thirty or forty seconds, but all I could think about was I had my rifle upstairs and I had to get to it fast. That was my thought process at the time. It was like a natural reflex. Although I was facing the possibility of imminent death, the adrenaline I had from the situation just kept me running up those stairs even as a barrage of bullets rang over my head. All I could think about was shooting back.

Rewind to five minutes earlier. I had been warned by a childhood friend to get out of there. "Lamontt, get the fuck out of here right now," Pro Ball, aka Ballgame, shouted from a car he was a passenger in. Pro Ball knew my family and me since I was little when I lived off of Ocean View Boulevard. His younger brother, DB, and I were best friends when we were kids, and his brother Melle Mel was the person who gave me the gun to shoot Denver, though he didn't have an idea who I was planning to shoot.

Pro Ball's family and mine had remained close even after I moved to East Dago. Although most people would have taken heed to Pro Ball's warning to get out of there, especially considering I knew he was a reputable gang member who wouldn't say something like that un- less he was serious, I was cocky, and probably drunk, which always lessened my inhibitions and made my actions even more irrational.

This was the way most gang members acted. You always had to post up, as we called it, no matter what danger you were in. One of us could get shot or shot at or even hear a rumor about a rival planning to come through and attack us, but it was almost mandatory that you still hung out or post up. You could never let the other side know you weren't willing to put it all on the line. It was gang machismo, but as I think on it now, it was stupidity most of us had, just like when Lunnie Dunnie had run up on me back when I was first trying to get put on with the East Dago Mob. I had to stay outside and post up at Highland Park right after that encounter. If I hadn't it could have been interpreted that I was scared and not a rida and you never wanted that jacket on you. Basically come outside and stay outside, no matter what, and even in the midst of a gang war, that's what you did.

To this day I really don't know what I was thinking that night and why I didn't react differently when I got a warning to leave. Obviously Pro Ball didn't tell me what was about to happen, but he cared enough about me to warn me that my life and the life of the others out there with me were in jeopardy. Well maybe he didn't care about anyone else out there but me.

He had been in the first car on a reconnaissance mission to see who was out there posted up, and within a minute or so I would find out that even if Pro Ball cared about my life, he obviously didn't care about whoever else was out there, and if I didn't heed the warning, that was on me and my own stupidity.

After the car Pro Ball was in pulled off, I became more alert, but I didn't give it much thought. As I said, it was about posting up, and even in that situation I was going to stay out and hang with my boys. Not more than three minutes later three cars came speeding down the street on 44th Street and then a barrage of bullets started coming from the cars in the direction of everyone who was standing in front of the apartments.

After a minute or so and my failed attempt to make it upstairs to my sister Rhonda's to get my gun to exchange gunfire, it was over. The cars left, and miraculously no one was hit by any of the bullets. If anyone should have been shot that night, it should have been me. Not only was I not smart enough to listen to Pro Ball's warning, but I also risked my life by not taking cover but instead running in front of the gunfire while attempting to retrieve my gun from upstairs at Rhonda's. Everyone out there that night was lucky.

We were either really fast runners, exceptionally quick bullet dodgers, or the guys shooting at us were horrible shots. At any rate, it was not the first or the last time I would be shot at, but it was definitely one of the more memorable experiences.

You may be wondering why a childhood friend of mine such as Pro Ball would attempt to kill my friends and me, I wondered too. He didn't want to kill me, because he had come by first on a reconnaissance mission to see who was out there. Pro Ball knew those were my homies out there and I was a member of the East Dago Mob, but he and the people he was with that night were on a kill mission, and I'm sure he assumed I would have gotten out of there after he warned me and I warned those around me. I did warn everyone to be on alert and was definitely aware that something could go down, but to understand why I didn't react in a way you would expect someone in that situation to react, you would have to understand the intricate mentality of an active gang member and the value or lack thereof that we place on our own lives as well as that of others.

Although East Dago Mob was rivals to a number of gangs and individuals, I wasn't quite sure why Pro Ball and his associates came through that particular night, but there was so much animosity going on at the time in the streets I know there was a legitimate street reason. I suspected it was in retaliation for something that went down with another drug organization that Pro Ball was down with. I don't think it was gang related per se, but who knows because there was so much shit going on in the streets around this time I couldn't keep track of everyone I was feuding with and why.

CHAPTER 11

Who's Plotting Against Me?

MY INTERACTIONS WITH Pro Ball and his family were not regular during this period of my life, but when we did interact, it seemed like it was impactful. His brother DB and I were always together back in the day, but when I moved away to the Four Corners, we remained friends, but stopped keeping in touch and hanging out like we used to.

After I had been in East Dago for a couple of years and had become a relatively successful drug dealer, I had clients from just about every black gang in San Diego coming to East Dago to buy drugs from me, which included Crips and Bloods and a number of them were from Ocean View. I was still cool with some of the guys from over there on Ocean View, especially the ones I was close to when I was little, such as Bubbly and his brother Charlie Bo who is now resting in peace, and of course DB and his brothers, Pro Ball and Melle Mel.

However, because I was banging East Dago Mob, some of those guys from Ocean View didn't like me, particularly because they felt like I switched sides or betrayed them. I hadn't lived over there since I was thirteen, but I can understand from a street mentality how some of them felt like I started off over there, but now my loyalty was the East Dago Mob.

Although DB and I hadn't been best friends in more than four or five years, I still considered him one of my closest friends. Whenever DB and I hung out, which wasn't often, we would clown around, smoke weed, and get drunk. DB was a real friend, and as we would say in the hood, "He was a real nigga to the core" and I knew I could trust him with my life. Even though some of DB's homies didn't like me, DB always kept it real with me and showed me love.

In fact, DB and I would occasionally have talks about issues some of his homies had with me because I was from East Dago Mob. He confirmed that since I started off over there with them when I was younger, some people thought my loyalty should have been with them. In true DB fashion, he didn't care I was in the East Dago Mob and told me he was glad. However, the animosity a few had for me would later play a role in a plot to rob me and also possibly kill me.

One night DB had come over to my spot to hang out with Cynthia and me. It was a night I had taken off from selling drugs, and Cynthia and I were just chillin', taking a night off from the hustle. Anyone who knew DB would attest he almost always had a smile, even if he was about to do something devious. I had known DB before he was allowed to come out of the house without his brothers, and he had never lost that look of innocence. He just had the kind of face that was seriously misleading for those who didn't know him.

On this particular night when DB came over, he looked pretty serious. He didn't have his typical all-fun-and-games look. I asked him if anything was wrong. To give just a little background on DB's street reputation, DB was a well- known active member from the 5/9 Brims gang off of Ocean View Boulevard in Southeast San Diego. He was one of the more active frontline lieutenants from over there, and the other hitters would confide in him about anything.

I knew it could have been anything bothering DB, because at that time there was so much going on in the streets, whether in East Dago or Southeast. It seemed like everyone was at war in 1988, whether from gangbangin' or fighting over drug territory. And when you include the gangs from L.A. and Compton that were trying to infiltrate San Diego's drug market, the late 1980s was a war zone.

When DB walked in the house he just gave me a look that only a street dude would recognize and immediately I asked Cynthia to leave the room. After Cynthia left the room, DB proceeded to tell me that he knew of some people who were planning to rob me and even mentioned possibly killing me. I could understand them maybe wanted to rob me because I had some money and large quantities of drugs, but killing me was personal because I was from East Dago Mob. It had been some years since I've been on that side of town, so the people talking about robbing me didn't know or didn't realize how close DB and his family and my family were.

DB told me he didn't think the dudes who were talking about me were going to really do anything, but he shut it down immediately anyway by making it known that I was off limits. He told them "Lamontt is my nigga." However, he still had concerns about some of his rogue homies and what they might do, and I did as well. I wasn't afraid though had my concerns. I had hitters in my circle who I knew would die or go to prison for life for me, so it was just that street shit you had to contend with. I also knew some of those dudes from Ocean View you would not want to run into in a dark alley no matter who you were. However, I knew DB and his brothers would never allow anyone to do anything to me if they could prevent it. I knew that even before Pro Ball warned me ahead of time that he and his crew were about to kill us. Well he didn't say those exact words, but pulling up in a car and yelling for me to get the fuck out of there right now was basically telling me he was about to light this block up with gunfire.

Around this time DB was on the run from the police and needed to get out of Southeast and lay low for a while. I trusted DB with my life. I trusted him around my girl and my unborn. And I trusted him around my money and drugs. So within a few days of our conversation he moved in with me and Cynthia and started working with me.

I can see it in my head like it happened today, but it happened nearly thirty years ago. DB had been working with me for about a week or so when one night we were chillin' in the house doing what we did, selling drugs. Clients were coming and going most of the night. On this particular night, lo and behold, at the door was one of the guys who had been dissing me and planning to rob me. He wasn't there to rob me but instead to buy some drugs, but the look on his face when he saw DB sitting there was classic. I'm sure DB was the last person he was expecting to see sitting in my living room. After the guy left, DB and I laughed about it for at least an hour.

I only mention this story to illustrate the love and respect DB and I had for each other, even though we weren't close like we were when we were kids and were from so-called rival neighborhoods. DB, just like his brother Pro Ball, probably saved my life. DB was one of the main hitters from his neighborhood and he was ridin' with me, his brother. Our friendship extended beyond the lapse of time or across gang lines.

One of the last conversations I had with DB before he stopped working with me and moved out was over the telephone around two o'clock in the morning. DB had taken one of my cars earlier in the day and said he was going to The South, another name for his neighborhood, to handle some business. Cynthia was around eight months pregnant with my son and she hated everyone, including DB and me, so she was pissed when I got a phone call from him in the middle of the night.

I knew DB was still on the run from the police and considering his reputation that call could have been related to just about any-thing. About ten seconds into the phone call DB told me the Green Machine, which was what we called the car he took, an old 1970s dark green Buick Skylark, had blown up on the freeway. I knew the Green Machine was a bucket, which is what we called older or less expensive cars we used only for making daily runs around town, but its blowing up on the freeway was a shock to me. I guess it shouldn't have been a shock, since the car was an old bucket, but to hear that the car had blown up definitely threw me off and was a first for me. I knew DB wasn't lying because he didn't have to. He could have told me he was drunk and crashed it. Or he had got into a high speed chase and crashed. It really didn't matter what happened as long as he was okay. For the next ten minutes DB and I laughed on the phone about the car blowing up while listening to eight-months-pregnant Cynthia lying next to me in the bed cussing me out, telling me to shut the fuck up or get off the phone.

After that call I never had a chance to find out exactly what happened that night that caused the car to explode on the freeway. I guess we were laughing so hard about the car blowing up that DB never got out exactly what happened. This happened around November 1988 and was one of the last in-depth conversations I had with DB. I don't know what DB was doing on that freeway that night, but knowing DB, it was probably something straight out the Wild, Wild, West. If anyone is reading this and knows what happened that night the Green Machine blew up, holla at your boy. I'm sure, or I hope, the statute of limitations has already run against anyone who is still living.

Rest in Heaven, DB, aka Fatt Daddy, my dude Derek.

CHAPTER 12

Christmas Night Tragedy

I WOULDN'T SAY I was rich, and in fact there were a number of drug dealers around East Dago and throughout Southeast who had a lot more money than I had, but at eighteen years old I probably had more money than most San Diego and Los Angeles drug dealers who were my age. I was gradually selling more and more weight and my connections of purchasing large amounts of drugs were getting better. I had enough money to live a relatively luxurious life. I had a posh townhouse. I owned two BMWs. I could eat dinner at any restaurant I wanted to. I could buy expensive clothes and jewelry. I was finally living my dream as an up-and-coming baller. I got the most thrill and satisfaction, however, from my gang activities. The money was great and I wanted more, but the excitement of the streets gave me a sense of invincibility, but I knew death was likely imminent if I didn't go to prison first. Death was around the corner and I was becoming more and more hardened to the streets each day.

The numbness to the streets and accompanied violence that I had experienced since I was about seven years old had culminated in who I was and who I was becoming. I loved my family. I loved my homies. I respected those who were civilians and not in the game. But I was becoming heartless toward anyone I perceived as an enemy. The only thing I cared about was becoming a rich drug dealer and earning a serious reputation as a gang member. In the back of my mind I knew the fun would eventually run out sooner or later. The money. The girls. Kicking it with the homies. The freedom just being alive. I knew my days were numbered.

It was Christmas night 1988. My life as a reputable gang member, LB Gunsmoke, and drug dealer, would skyrocket over a couple years but have a precipitous fall almost overnight. It was a normal night for me, besides being Christmas. We had already done the exchanging of gifts and hanging out with family and friends for the holiday. Cynthia was nine months pregnant and was relaxing upstairs reading, while I entertained some of my homies downstairs. We were hanging out in my soon-to-be-born son's nursery drinking and exchanging war stories.

Cynthia was ready to give birth any day, so I tried not to venture off for too long but continued to run the streets as much as I ever did. The fact that it was Christmas didn't change my friends' and my daily rituals. We would spend some time with our families earlier in the day but would reassemble later, and on this night we got together at my house.

After a couple of hours of drinking downstairs, several of us decided to go to the liquor store to get some more forties of Olde English 800 and Cisco and Super Socco and Gin. Although I had money and could buy Hennessey or some other expensive cognac, when I was with my little homies I kept it gangsta. We were 8-ball junkies*.

It was four of us, Choo Choo, Baby T, T-Nut, and me. We all had become close since the days as street hustlers on 44th Street and attending Hoover High School. Baby T and I were the oldest, at eighteen, and had known each other since our days on the Four Corners when Baby T was an active Ghost Town Crip. Choo Choo and T-Nut were younger at sixteen and fifteen, respectively. We knew we had a lot of enemies and were in a serious war with two gangs in particular, so we never went anywhere without at least two of us carrying some kind of firearm. However, this was Christmas night, and we had planned to just hang out around the house and chill. We weren't too concerned with getting into any drama that night. In fact we were just going to make a quick liquor store run to Christine's Liquor, in our own neighborhood, and then return home. Besides, Cynthia was ready to burst, and although I still ran the streets, I knew I had to stay close and therefore wasn't doing as much as I would normally do. Even though we had anticipated a quick and uneventful run to the liquor store, like so many other times before, in my neighborhood nothing could be guaranteed to be uneventful.

As we pulled up to the liquor store there were two or three cars already parked in the lot. We instantly recognized the cars as belonging to 4 Tray Gangsters. Of course we could have easily just driven away and gone to another store, but why would we do that? This was our neighborhood. We had a lot of machismo and gang arrogance and would not allow anyone to keep us away from the liquor we considered ours. We went to the store that night in my car. I was driving. My pride wouldn't allow me to keep driving past Christine's Liquor. Besides, something in me said, "Okay, it is Christmas night and nobody, not even our enemies, wants any drama tonight. In hindsight, I should have kept driving.

The plan was to get out, get our alcohol, and leave without any issues. After I parked my car we all got out and headed into the store. As soon as we entered the store, words were exchanged between our two groups and a confrontation ensued. Choo Choo and T-Nut kept telling the store clerk really loud, so that the rival gang members could hear, that we were going to buy forty-four forty ounces of Olde English. Forty-four was the number that represented our clique, 44 Blocc Hustlers. By then T-Nut and one of the rivals were in a one-on-one heated argument near the front entrance. It was probably about six of them and it was the four in my group, so although we weren't evenly matched, we weren't largely outnumbered, either.

After a couple of minutes the argument became more intense, and I knew if it was not deescalated real quickly it could get out of hand. However, a strange thing happened as T-Nut and the other guy kept arguing. One of the rivals who was closer to my age and one of their shot callers, and I looked at each other and started laughing, shaking our heads. We knew each other well and were definitely archenemies, but when you've been in the streets and around gang violence long enough, you can tell when someone doesn't really want any issue. I think that night neither of us wanted any problem. I also knew if we ever had to retaliate against them and they went back to L.A., my homies from Grape Street Watts Crips already told us that they would take us to the 4 Tray's neighborhood on the Eastside of L.A. where their neighborhood was located, because we didn't know our way around the back streets of L.A.

Like so many times in those situations, unfortunately, no one wanted to take the high road, and that almost always led to something horribly going wrong, and that night would be no different. No one on either side did anything to escalate the situation that was occurring with T-Nut and the other guy until we all got outside. Everyone started walking to their cars, getting ready to leave. As we were all getting into our cars realizing we avoided something that could have potentially gotten really ugly really fast, one of the other guys stood outside of his car demanding that T-Nut fight his friend, I guess since they were the first and last ones arguing.

By that time everyone from both sides was in the cars getting ready to leave. I was already in the driver's seat and T-Nut was in the backseat. The only person who was still out of the car and in front of my car now was the guy insisting that there be a fight between T-Nut and his boy. He knew that I was older and one of the shot callers for my younger homies, so he kept telling me as he stood in front of my car to tell T-Nut to get out and fight his homie one on one.

It shouldn't have been a surprise to me how this dude was acting. He was about six feet five inches and known to be a bully and thought he was tough, but the word on the street he was a basketball player in Los Angeles and only played a tough guy when he moved to San Diego. No one was afraid of him, and we all thought he was just a big, soft giant. At any rate, after a couple of minutes of insisting that T-Nut get out of the car and fight his little homie, I had had enough. I told T-Nut to get out of the car and whoop this dude's homie's ass real quick so we could leave. Everyone exited their cars and immediately started throwing punches, and then it was an all-out brawl in the parking lot of "our" liquor store.

Although the fight was uneven because there were at least six of them against four of us, it didn't seem to be too uneven or that they were even getting the best of us. I had a gun on me, I know Baby T had a gun on him, but I didn't think Choo Choo or T-Nut had any weapons. I figured the guys we were fighting had guns as well. I mean during this time and considering we were at war with each other, at least one person would be packing a pistol, or it would be gangbanging malpractice.

Initially I thought shots were just fired in the air and kept fighting, but it didn't take long for me to realize T-Nut had just shot one of the guys he was fighting.

T-Nut was only fifteen years old. I was eighteen and a little bigger than him at the time, and from what I recall he was the youngest of everyone out there. I'm sure because we were outnumbered and we were fighting some big dudes, T-Nut felt that the other guys were getting the best of us and he did what he had to do. T-Nut also saw one of the other guys flash a gun, which I suspect he believed it was about to escalate to the next level. I admit I was shocked T-Nut pulled out a gun and shot someone at point blank range. I guess I shouldn't have been shocked considering we had homies younger than him already putting in work for the Mob, including his younger brother Lil Pimp, who was only twelve years old. Back in the '80s if you weren't down with the frontline action or money makin', you weren't considered a real East Dago Mobstas, and it didn't matter how young you were as long as you were old enough to hang out. I know that probably sounds stupid, but we didn't look at it that way. It was just our way of life unfortunately. If you weren't raised in it, *you could never understand it.*

Later that night we would learn that the guy who got shot died from his injuries. I knew after that night there was going to be a lot of violence to come. They were from 4 Tray Gangsters a really big gang in Los Angeles, and the person who died was a beloved member.

I still harbor a lot of guilt from that night. Not only did someone lose his life, but I also feel that since I was the driver and one of the oldest, I could have kept driving and not stop, or I should have never told T-Nut to get out the car to fight in the first place. T-Nut looked up to me and I let him down. In a way I blame myself more than anyone else for that night. That night cost everyone in my car a lot, but what we lost pales in comparison to losing your life. I admit back then I didn't have a lot of sympathy for anyone I considered my enemy. Today, however, it eats me up every day knowing I could have done something to prevent that tragedy that night. I couldn't let my ego be suppressed for one night, not even on Christmas night, when I had a child due any day. I've made some bad decisions in my life that I regret, and this is one at the top. I was the getaway driver of the car and an accessory to murder. And after that night, my life would never be the same. I own my past.

If you weren't there you probably won't believe what happened next. As we used to say when referring to an enemy we were looking forward to running into, "It was on on sight." This meant whenever and wherever you saw that person, it was going down. The particular person we ran into had been on our radar and was someone we considered an imminent threat. Literally minutes after the brawl and shooting at Christine's Liquor, and before we made it back safely to my townhouse, we were in a shootout with a rival gang member from Emerald Hills Bloods. Once my car pulled up next to his, gun fire immediately was exchanged, but fortunately for everyone involved no one was hit. What had started off as a quick liquor store run on Christmas night turned into one of the most memorable events of my life.

Once I got back home I just laid back with Cynthia, reflecting on what had just happened at the liquor store and on the way home. Cynthia wasn't due for a few weeks, so I wasn't expecting any labor surprises that night. All I wanted to do was relax and then gather my thoughts. I knew that what I thought was a gang war was nothing in comparison to what was about to go down. I was about to bring a baby into the world, and I loved Cynthia and cared for her safety. For at least the rest of the night I was going to try to relax as much as I could and figure out some things.

After just having a fight with a rival gang that left one man dead, and then minutes later getting into a shootout with another rival gang, Cynthia decided to go into labor on the same night. Talk about less than ideal timing! I knew at least two gangs were out looking for me from two separate shootings early in the evening. My life was in grave danger and now I had to get up and go out in the middle of the night with my girlfriend who was in labor and about to give birth to my child.

I knew I couldn't take Cynthia to the hospital in the same car I was driving earlier that night, so I decided to take her to the hospital in my 1963 Impala, which was recognizable from a mile away. It was around one in the morning with hardly any other cars out on the road, so I would be conspicuous regardless of what I drove.

Cynthia and I were living in our townhouse in the heart of East Dago on Marlborough Street right off of University Avenue. There weren't many backstreets on the way to UCSD hospital in Hillcrest, which was about ten minutes away, so I figured most of the drive would be on one of the main streets.

I knew that my rivals were likely out looking for my homies and me on any given night, but this particular night I was certain they were out on the hunt. As I was driving to the hospital looking over my shoulder and glaring at every single car that passed me, when I thought it couldn't get any worse while Cynthia was screaming hysterically from her labor pains, I looked at my fuel gauge, and it was on empty. There was nothing else I could do but pull over at the nearest gas station.

Although I had a couple of guns on me, I was terrified. I wasn't necessarily afraid for myself, but I was with my pregnant girlfriend and my unborn child. I could accept my fate whatever that was, but I knew any attempt on my life could possibly harm Cynthia and my unborn child, who could easily get caught in crossfire. If that happened and I survived I could never forgive myself. Fortunately I was able to stop at the Shell station on 40th and University Avenue within a few blocks, pump my gas really quickly, and continue to the hospital.

Even now there are times I think about that night and get chills. I had to watch my back for killers I knew were looking for me while pumping gas in the middle of the night with my pregnant girlfriend in labor. We eventually made it to the hospital safely, but the terrifying night was far from over.

After the doctor examined Cynthia he determined that she wasn't dilating enough, and he sent us home. The ride home wasn't as scary as going to the hospital, but it was tense nonetheless. Once we got home Cynthia seemed fine; we believed that maybe it was just a false alarm. However, within an hour or so after we were home, Cynthia started screaming once again from labor pains.

Although I tried to talk Cynthia out of going back to the hospital, as if that was going to stop her labor pain, we got up and I drove her once again back to the hospital. It was now about three in the morning, and it seemed like every person in every car that passed us looked like one of the guys from the fight earlier or from the shoot-out. Paranoia was an understatement. Once we arrived at the hospital the second time I told the doctor to keep her until she gave birth. My son Marion Lamontt Bowens, Jr., was born several hours later on December 26, 1988. One life was taken earlier on Christmas night and one came into existence the following day, both related to each other in a strange way.

R.I.P. Playboy from 4-Tray Gangsta Crip.

Believe it or not there were times during those tumultuous years when I was deeply entrenched in gangbanging and drug dealing that I thought about a peaceful life free of crime. My dreams of becoming a big-time drug dealer were often paralleled with a dream of having a legitimate, successful career, although I didn't know what kind of legitimate, successful career I wanted, but nonetheless I knew it was crime-free and didn't involve gangs. Unfortunately this parallel thinking would wither away almost as soon as it came, because my situation didn't give me a lot of time to dream about shit that wasn't even minutely close to my reality. After I got my head out the clouds for that couple of minutes or so, I would have my reality check and then refocus all of my energy on the task at hand, which was gangbanging and making money selling drugs. It was as if I had these periodic and brief dreams of life as a model citizen just to cleanse my soul from all the bullshit I was experiencing daily. No matter what positive thoughts occasionally came to mind, ultimately I couldn't see past the despair I was living.

After the tragic events of Christmas night and the blessing of my son being born early the following morning, my life didn't change drastically. I was young, dumb, and too naïve to make any positive changes in my life. I was an East Dago Mobsta resigned to whatever fate came with my gang membership and my drug kingpin ambitions. What I didn't know at the time was fate was approaching a lot sooner than I realized.

Rest well in heaven, Choo Choo, aka Gerald.

CHAPTER 13

It's a Raid!

ABOUT A WEEK or so after the Christmas night shootings and the birth of my son, I was driving at night by myself on 44th Street about to turn onto University Avenue when I spotted around ten cars full of guys from 4 Tray Gangsters. They had just lost one of their beloved members, and I knew they were out looking for my boys and me. I understood that they would be out for revenge, but damn, I wasn't expecting them to bring their whole neighborhood down from L.A. I made a quick turn onto a back street so they wouldn't see me and then I called my homies to let them know we were seriously at war. I knew from that point it was on.

I had also been warned a couple of days before by an associate of ours named Craig Mack who was from West Coast Rollin 30s Crips. Craig Mack was good friends with and worked for one of East Dago Mob's generals, Charlie Steele, aka Big CS. Craig Mack told me that he had run into one of the L.A. gang members from 4 Tray and he had told him that whenever they saw me, whether it was inside a 7-Eleven, Kmart, or McDonald's, in broad daylight or at night, they were going to kill me. Of course hearing this news only pumped me up and increased my adrenaline. In a sick and twisted ghetto way that only a serious gangbanger or former gangbanger could understand, knowing that I had reached a level that I was that nigga people wanted to kill, stroked my ego.

DON'T LET YOUR PAST HOLD YOU BACK

I was at home chillin' with Baby T when I heard a knock on the door. Baby T and I were upstairs drinking our usual forty ounces of Olde English 800 mixed with Cisco and exchanging war stories, probably. I didn't think much of it when I went to the door, but I always asked who it was and looked through the peephole. When I asked who was there, the person on the other side said a name I was familiar with, but I knew the voice didn't match the name. Also, the peephole had been obscured, and I couldn't see who was at the door. My mental antenna instantly went up, and I ran upstairs and grabbed one of my guns and ran back downstairs to the door. I asked one more time, "Who's at the door?" The person repeated the same name. By this time Baby T realized what was going on and grabbed the sawed-off double barrel twelve-gauge and climbed out the upstairs window onto the rooftop to surprise whoever was at the door on the other side. I cocked the gun back really loud so whoever was at the door could hear it and waited for Baby T to make it outside and to the front door. I was waiting to either hear gunshots or Baby T's voice at the door. About forty seconds after Baby T went out the upstairs window, I could hear him at the door saying, "Lamontt, they left."

To this day I don't know who was at my door that night. I knew it would be sooner rather than later that the Grim Reaper would be paying me a visit. Sadly, even though my life was in more peril than it had ever been in, as long as I was the biggest drug dealer I could be and a reputable gang member, the nigga that everyone wanted to kill, I was still willing to take the risks—even if it meant death. In fact, for many of us living the kind of life I was living at the time, dying for one's gang was the ultimate sacrifice and honor. As sick and ignorant as it may sound getting killed wasn't something you sought out, but you embraced the possibility because you knew it came with the territory, and you believed that you'd be a martyr, a legend in your hood. A sad way of thinking, but that was my reality.

I thought I had finally reached the pinnacle of my ghetto existence.

I wasn't the biggest drug dealer or the toughest gang member, but I could hold my own. I was LB Gunsmoke, from East Dago Mob. Considering where I started off, first at seven years old watching my brothers and their friend count money just stolen from an armored truck, then being ten years old in Bakersfield trying to emulate my sisters boyfriends who were older gang members, to my days on Ocean View Boulevard and experiencing street violence like never before, all the way to my years struggling and dreaming to become a baller on the Four Corners of Death and 44th Street, I had finally arrived.

I had money, most of the material things I wanted, and status in my neighborhood. I was either revered or hated, and I was fine with either. And I still had ambition to go a lot higher in the dope game. I was living reckless and on the edge. I was living the bad life of a crack cocaine dealer and East Dago Mob lieutenant who ran in the circles of the captains and generals. However, what I didn't know at the time was that my steady and consistent rise over the past few years would pale in comparison to my fall. The life that I had become accustomed to would come to an abrupt end on the morning of January 25, 1989. Maybe it literally and figuratively saved my life.

There were homicide detectives, uniformed police officers, Anti-Gang Task Force, and San Diego County Sheriff Deputies, all pounding on my front door simultaneously. It was around seven o'clock in the morning, and initially I didn't know who was knocking. All I heard was a continuous loud pounding. My first reaction was to grab one of the six or seven guns I had stored under my bed and prepare for war. It was either a robbery attempt or my enemies coming all out to get me. For some reason I never thought it would be the police, which was strange considering all the drugs I was selling and the number of gang activities I was involved in.

I don't recall which gun I grabbed, or if I grabbed more than one, but with at least one gun in tow, I went downstairs to investigate the commotion at my front door. Being who I was, I knew I had to always be prepared for someone coming either to try to kill me or rob me or both. I had already had several of my houses riddled with bullets in the past and because of a previous failed attempt at a home invasion, I rarely answered my door without being prepared for anything.

On this day, however, by the time I was halfway down the stairs to investigate the continuous knocking and yelling from outside, it became apparent really fast who awaited me on the other side. My brother, his wife, and their young daughter had been in town visiting me from Virginia, and they were sleeping in my downstairs bedroom. This was probably the only time I can say I was happy that I had been an arrogant jerk to Cynthia, because she left me a couple of weeks earlier and took my newborn son with her, so they weren't there to experience this event. Unfortunately my brother and his family were.

As the police continued pounding on the door, their demands for me to open the door became more and more urgent. I refused to open the door. I ran back upstairs, put my gun or guns back under the bed while the police continued to attempt to break through the front door. I figured it was time for me to make my escape.

My safe was in my bedroom closet, so I opened it, grabbed all my money, placed it in a trash bag, and went to my kitchen window that led to the side of my townhouse with a bunch of trees. I got ready to jump out the window, but to my surprise, when I looked down, several law enforcement officers were pointing guns at me. I immediately ran to my balcony window, the same window Baby T had climbed out of to surprise whoever was at my door that other night. Once I got to the window and looked out of it, once again, more police were pointing their guns right at me from below. I then realized my house was surrounded and there would be no escaping.

In telling this story it sounds like I had five or ten minutes to do all this running around, but in reality it was probably less than two or three minutes. Everything happened fast and I was moving like my life depended on it. I had enough time to reflect on my life, though. As I thought about my next move, I knew it was all over for me. I didn't know what the cops were there for, but many things came across my mind. My entire life for the previous two years flashed in front of me.

My townhouse had a thick reinforced door that wasn't easy to break down and the cops didn't come with a battering ram, but I knew I was trapped. After pausing for a few seconds to gather my thoughts after going to the last window and still listening to the cops trying to break through my front door, I still had time to put my money back in the safe and walk downstairs to open the front door.

By this time, however, my brother got tired of the banging. He likely feared for his wife's and daughter's safety had the cops broken down the door and not knowing what was awaiting them on the other side, so he finally opened the door for them. With dozens of weapons pointed at our heads, the cops handcuffed my brother and me.

All this commotion was over the Christmas night shooting at the liquor store that had occurred a month earlier. My house was being raided and searched for any evidence related to the murder. The search warrant detailed a search for any evidence related to what occurred on Christmas night, particularly the murder weapon and any gang paraphernalia. They were making a simultaneous raid on all four of us who were there that night, so as they were raiding my house, they were also raiding T-Nut's house, Baby T's house, and Choo Choo's house.

During the raid the cops asked me to open my safe. Although I could have given the police a difficult time and made them take the safe to their headquarters and break it open, I realized that it was all over for me, so for once I wouldn't be an asshole to the police. I had done

109

enough of that since I was thirteen years old. At that point being a jerk would not give me any satisfaction or benefit me in any way. Once the safe was open, the police counted all of the money in front of me while I was handcuffed in the upstairs living room sitting on the floor. About a dozen or so other police searched the entire house.

The police eventually seized the money found in the safe as well as one of my BMWs parked in my driveway. Fortunately for me none of my other cars were on the premises at the time, or they too would have been seized. About a couple of hours after the raid had begun I was taken from my townhouse and booked into the county jail. They didn't arrest my brother or his wife because they were not the subjects of the raid and were on vacation visiting from Virginia.

Although I had at least six or seven guns under my bed at the time of the raid, none of them was the murder weapon, and the police ended up charging me with two counts of possession of a deadly weapon because I possessed a sawed-off shotgun and sawed-off M-1 rifle with an extended magazine. Ironically, the guns I was charged with were the exact same kind of guns Dave and I had purchased from Kmart a couple of years earlier when we had that issue with Lunnie Dunnie. I was also initially charged with accessory to murder.

CHAPTER 14

The End of an Era

ALTHOUGH I WAS making preparations to make bail, I didn't think it was urgent initially. After a day or two in jail I was resigned to the fact that I was going to prison for a long time. The day had finally arrived. Just about everyone I associated with had done some time. I had even been to juvenile hall a few times and to the county jail a number of times for gun possession, but this time I knew I was going to the penitentiary, the big-boy graduation time that all the youngsters in the hood anticipated happening eventually. When it came to prison, it wasn't a matter of if; it was a matter of when. It was a way of life and a rite of passage. I had just turned nineteen a couple weeks earlier, and I was on my way to prison for serious weapons charges and accessory to murder.

After a couple of days in jail I was visited by my attorney, Kate Coyne, who was representing me from the Public Defenders Office. During that first visit she droppped a bomb on me. She told me that she was informed that I, along with several members of the East Dago Mob, among a number of other individuals from Southeast and East San Diego, were under a secret indictment that had not yet been unsealed. Receiving this news would be bad for anyone at any time, but for me it was horrible news, considering I was already facing serious chargers in state court and had to prepare myself for likely dozens of years in prison.

Attorney Kate Coyne, who I would soon learn was an excellent criminal defense attorney, suggested that I bail out immediately before the federal indictment was unsealed, and if I didn't, I risked doing all the years I faced in state prison first and then would have to do whatever federal prison sentence I received after I was released from state prison. Say what you want about Public Defenders, they are some of the best, the brightest, and most rigorous attorneys, and Kate Coyne was no exception. Although the feds seized most of my money, I could have asked Dave or Big Boo Gist to get me a private lawyer, but I already had one of the best. She knew it would be better for me to go to federal prison and have my state prison sentence run concurrently with my federal sentence. Even though what my attorney was telling me was confusing and I didn't completely understand, I understood enough that I needed to get out of there right away.

I called Dave right after my visit with my attorney and he told me he would get me bailed out immediately. He got in contact with Junior, my former boss, and my homie Big Boo Gist, and they got the money and property to secure my release within a day. With the serious state charges pending and the inevitable federal indictment coming soon, I knew that if somehow I got lucky and beat one of the cases, I'd still lose and was going to prison for a long time, whether it was state prison or federal prison.

Because Cynthia and I weren't on good terms after she moved out, I wanted to get away and spend some time with her and my newborn son before I went away to prison. I felt guilty about what happened between Cynthia and me, and I didn't want to go away to prison on bad terms.

Although I was out on bail, I knew that once the federal indictment came out, my bail from the state charge would likely be revoked and I would be sitting in the federal Metropolitan Correctional Center (MCC) until I was on my way to the federal penitentiary. I just wanted to spend some time with Cynthia and my baby before I was locked away.

I was released on a Wednesday morning from the county jail and had a preliminary hearing scheduled for that Friday morning. I didn't want to skip my hearing and risk getting my bail revoked, so I planned to attend the hearing on Friday and then leave immediately after with Cynthia and Lamontt Jr. for the weekend. The weekend getaway would basically be a good-bye weekend, because although I didn't know when the federal indictment was coming out, I knew it could be any day. All I hoped was to make it through Friday morning's hearing so I could leave town for the weekend. I just wanted that final weekend.

I got up Friday morning as planned and went downtown to for my court appearance on my state charges. The only good news that came out of that hearing was the district attorney's office deciding not to bring charges for accessory to murder. But I would still face trial for the deadly weapons seized. My temporary good fortune would last only a few minutes, because I soon found out the federal indictment had been unsealed.

Toward the end of the Friday morning hearing I noticed two men enter the courtroom wearing suits. I knew attorneys wear suits, but they didn't look like attorneys. I had an instant bad feeling that they were the feds coming to get me. I watched as the two men walked over to one of the deputies and talked to him. As soon as the proceeding was over, the two men walked over to me and handcuffed me. They were US marshals and one of the deputies had informed them that I was present in the courtroom. I was arrested in the courtroom and immediately taken to MCC in downtown San Diego, where I would remain for the next eight months before being sent to federal prison.

During the first few months at MCC I was escorted periodically to San Diego Superior Court for various hearings related to the possession of deadly weapons charge. Because I listened to my attorney and bailed out before the federal indictment was unsealed, after a few months the state offered me a plea deal that would allow my state sentence to run concurrently with any federal sentence. The assistant district attorney knew I was facing an uphill battle in federal court with very serious federal drug crimes under the mandatory minimum drug sentencing guidelines, so I'm sure they assumed I would do at least the minimum amount of time the plea bargain recommended, two-and-a-half years. I believe that even if I had beaten the federal charge, which would have been a near impossibility because the feds rarely lose, the state could have rearrested me and forced me to serve out any remaining time left on my sentence.

Although everything appeared to look dire to me, even though it wasn't, I had to feel a little bit fortunate that I was not facing accessory to murder and I was able to have my state and federal sentences run concurrently. However, upon my release, which at that point seemed very far in the future, I would still have two serious felony convictions on my permanent record—one from the state and one from the feds and all the baggage that would accompany it—for the rest of my life.

The first time I met with my attorney for my federal case was sometime in early February 1989. The indictment had been unsealed in late January and I had been in federal custody since my arrest on that fateful Friday a week or so before. During our visit my attorney gave me a copy of the federal indictment on me that was at least a hundred pages long.

There were twenty-two named defendants in the indictment, and my name was listed as number twenty two.* I don't think there was any particular rhyme or reason behind the order of names on the indictment, considering I was probably a bigger drug dealer than at least six or seven people on the list; however, the ordering of the top ten or eleven people on the indictment made more sense to me than the last ten. After the top ten people on the indictment, I believe the feds just started adding names of people they suspected of participating in major drug transactions in East Dago and Southeast. Nonetheless, I actually believe that being the last person listed on the indictment helped me by giving the perception that I wasn't one of the higher-ups such as a captain or lieutenant in a drug conspiracy and therefore a small fry, which I had no problem with. It wasn't like I was going to ask the prosecutor to move my name up a few places.

Because of the crack cocaine epidemic that devastated inner-city communities across the country, Congress passed some extremely harsh mandatory drug sentencing laws for crack cocaine. For most federal crack cocaine cases of the time, the minimum amount of prison for the smallest amount of crack was ten years. Although I had seen the devastation of crack cocaine on my community, I know if all crack cocaine dealers had been predominately white instead of black, Congress would have never passed such harsh and archaic drug sentencing laws for nonviolent drug offenses.

For possessing only two ounces of crack cocaine coupled with the conspiracy charge, I was initially facing a minimum mandatory sentence of forty years to life in federal prison. At the time I could have been in possession of a kilogram of powered cocaine and would have been facing a lot less time, but crack cocaine was the boogeyman in America, and I was caught up in the rapture of the so-called "war on drugs."* It was a time when politicians used poor and working-class black people as scapegoats for the social ills of society, and then enacted draconian mandatory-minimum drug sentencing laws that was the impetus of the Age of Mass Incarceration* which devastated more black families for at least a generation than crack cocaine itself.

I wasn't charged with murder. I wasn't charged with assaulting anyone with a deadly weapon. I wasn't even considered one of the major drug dealers in my indictment, so how could I be facing forty years to life for my first offense, and I use first offense loosely, because it was the first time I had gotten caught for anything serious, at nineteen years old.

One can only imagine my shock as well as fear when I initially heard the amount of time I was facing—forty years to life. I was familiar with people receiving sentences like the one I was facing if they were convicted of murder or were a drug kingpin, but for selling drugs at my level, it was unbelievable for me. I was a peon in comparison to the head guy in my indictment, Rob Dog. At best I was a small-fry compared to my top ten codefendants. I don't care how much of a gangster one thinks he or she is or how many times one has been to prison, facing that much time would frighten the hell out of anyone.

During my first month or so in federal custody, I had become terrified of the federal government. In fact it seemed like the accessory-to-murder charge in state court paled in comparison to going up against the feds. After several months and numerous court hearings and amendment after amendment to the indictment, what initially felt like a dire situation started to look a little brighter for me. After consulting with my attorney over a number of months, I realized that if I accepted responsibility and pleaded guilty, I was likely facing a minimum mandatory sentence of only ten years in prison. Yes, "only" ten years.

Ten years in prison sounded a helluva lot better than a minimum mandatory sentence of forty years, however, if I took my chances and went to trial and was convicted, there was a possibility I would never come home. It didn't mean that if I took my chances at trial and lost the judge would sentence me to forty years, but considering the propensity for prison violence while serving a twenty-year or longer sentence, anything could happen, especially considering I was only nineteen at the time and a gang member.

Even though accepting responsibility and pleading guilty was becoming a real possibility for me, I still didn't have a lot of hope for receiving a light sentence, considering my judge, U.S. District Court Judge William Enwright, was notorious for being tough and handing out harsh sentences for drug-related crimes. Nonetheless, leading up to my trial date, I held out hope that the prosecutor would offer me a plea agreement not seeking more than several years. I was dreaming and expecting too much, but I figured it was my first offense, or at least the first time I was prosecuted, and it would be my first time going to prison. I was only nineteen years old and wasn't considered a captain or lieutenant. I couldn't fathom doing ten or more years in prison for selling drugs. I always knew when I was gangbanging that the possibility of being involved in a violent situation could potentially put me away for life, but I had no idea how the federal government operated concerning drug trafficking. But I wasn't a kingpin. I didn't even know half the people on my indictment.

As my trial date was approaching, out of the blue and to my surprise, I would have one "get-out-of-jail-free card." I admit short of snitching on my codefendants I would have never thought that I would be offered a way out of the mess I had gotten myself into. I couldn't believe it when my get-out-of-of-jail free card was brought to me in MCC by my attorney for my federal case.

Usually when an inmate at MCC got a regular attorney visit, you would go into the regular visiting room and sit at your own table and discuss your case with your attorney. This is what had occurred with me for more than five or six months while being locked up in MCC. Whenever the correctional officers came to get me for my attorney visit, I'd be brought into the visiting room with everyone else. Sometimes there would be other inmates visiting with their family members, and at other times inmates would be meeting with their attorneys.

One particular Saturday afternoon would be totally different. When I was told I had an attorney visit and to get ready, I assumed I would be led out into the main visiting room like usual. The correctional officer instead put me in an elevator and took me to a floor I had never been on before. We went down the elevator maybe six or seven floors, and when it stopped and we got off, I was led into a locked room. I was baffled. I didn't ask any questions, but I definitely didn't know what was going on. I can't recall if I was nervous, but I definitely was confused. The correctional officer locked the door behind me and there was no one else in the room except my attorney sitting at a table. My attorney told me to have a seat while he was looking at some papers on the table in front of him. After about two minutes of small talk, he got to the point of this "top secret" attorney/client visit.

My attorney looked at me with a straight face as he showed me four names written on a piece of paper. He told me that the district attorney's office told him that if I helped them solve the murders of those four people on that piece of paper they could help me with my federal case. I was blown away. I never would have expected that offer. Of course I was familiar with the names on the paper. I remember verbatim what I told my attorney about a second after he relayed to me what the district attorney's offer to me was. I looked at him and said, "How can I help them if I don't know nothing?" I also remember verbatim what my attorney's response was. He gave me a smile and said, "I knew you were going to say that." That was the end of that meeting and the last time that conversation ever came up again.

Once I was back on my floor in MCC, I immediately told my codefendants that were in MCC with me what had just occurred and then relayed it to the streets by telephone. I knew that if I had any chance of getting out of doing some serious prison time, that chance ended once my attorney left that visiting room on that Saturday afternoon.

The first plea deal the prosecutor offered me was ten years in prison. This offer was within the minimum mandatory guidelines, and the prosecutor agreed to not ask the judge to sentence me to any more than the ten years if I pleaded guilty. Under the new sentencing guidelines it took all the power away from the judge and gave it to the prosecution. Although some judges went outside the guidelines or what the prosecution recommended, it was extremely rare, and their decision could be overturned for not following the law, so basically it was up to the prosecutor how much time a defendant would receive. For me the ten-year plea deal was unacceptable, and I declined the offer. I felt that I was too small of a dealer to face that amount of time for a "nonviolent" crime and first offense.

The final first holdout and showdown, for a lack of a better word, came in July 1989 right before I was scheduled to go to trial. I held out as long as I could for the best plea offer possible. I had a court hearing scheduled for later that afternoon, and I had been moved from the housing unit at MCC through the underground tunnel to the holding cell, which inmates called the holding tank, where they kept prisoners before entering the courtroom. Although I knew if I took my chances and went to trial I could receive a very long prison sentence, I was prepared to go to trial, and my attorney was in last-minute ne-gotiations with the prosecutor to see if he was willing to agree to a lower sentence.

During my attorney and the prosecutor's negotiation regarding my plea agreement, my attorney would come back to the holding tank where I was being held several times to inform me of the status of the negotiations. Finally, after around the third time coming back to talk to me, my attorney returned with a smirk on his face similar to the one he had when he responded to my answer about helping the district attorney solve some murders.

I remember wondering what the hell he was smiling about.

I was about to go to prison for a long time and had been sitting in a holding tank for hours, and this guy was smiling at me. I didn't see any reason to believe it was a happy moment unless all the charges were dismissed and the feds were releasing me or, as an alternative, I was only going to face only a few years. I would soon find out it was the latter, which was why my attorney was smiling.

After refusing to budge and agree to any deal that I felt was unacceptable, the prosecutor agreed that I would plead guilty and face no more than sixty-three to seventy-eight months in prison, which was the minimum mandatory guideline for simple possession of less than two ounces of crack cocaine and conspiracy. The prosecutor even agreed to ask the judge to sentence me to the lower end of the guidelines, which was sixty-three months. I don't think I ended up smiling with my attorney, but I was relieved. He did a good job. Thanks Attorney James Pokorny.

Although sixty-three to seventy-eight months in prison sounded like a better plea deal than a minimum mandatory ten-year sentence, I was still contemplating going to trial, because I knew if the witness didn't show up at trial to testify against me, there was no other strong evidence connecting me to any conspiracy. It would have basically boiled down to possession of crack cocaine, and if the person I had allegedly sold crack cocaine to would not show up to testify, I believed I could be acquitted.

Of course that was my naïve way of thinking at the time; however, I would soon get a reality check and realize that it wasn't that simple. Considering that I was facing the mighty power of the United States Government with a 90 percent conviction rate, coupled with likely being demonized as a black crack cocaine conspirator in front of a majority of white jurors, sixty-three months in prison didn't sound so bad.

I still couldn't get out of my head that EJ, who was like an uncle to me, was the person who was going to testify against me at my trial. I used to break dance for him at Ocean View Park back in 1983 when I was thirteen years old. He was the one who introduced me to major drug dealing when I was fifteen years old and helped inspire my dreams of becoming a kingpin. My whole family trusted him enough to allow me to spend weeks with him out of town selling drugs during the summer of 1985, and now he had turned on several of my co-conspirators and me. Because I was so close to him back in the day and trusted him, I was the one who had brought him into the East Dago Mob circle.

The irony of all of this was that EJ, who basically introduced me to selling crack cocaine, was now working as an informant for the DEA and would be the person to bring me down. I just couldn't imagine that EJ would testify against me and be responsible for sending me away to prison. Although I had become a relatively successful drug dealer, EJ had purchased only one controlled transaction from me that was monitored by the DEA, and it was for two ounces of crack cocaine back in October 1988. I actually felt somewhat lucky, considering he had purchased drugs from me on many occasions and in greater amounts. Nonetheless, I thought he was despicable for turning on me and several of my friends.

I was still contemplating refusing any plea agreement and instead taking my chances and going to trial, but my attorney advised me, and smartly so, that it was a huge risk. I sat in that holding tank for a few more minutes praying harder than I had to, at that point. I knew that if I accepted the plea agreement and got sixty-three months, which was a little more than five years, I would get out of prison while still in my early twenties. I wasn't happy, but I could live with that. Five years in prison may sound like an immense amount of time for most people, but considering the harsh minimum mandatory drug sentences for crack cocaine during that time, coupled with the reputation of the judge I had, who was known for giving out years for drug sentences as though they were weeks, I was getting a slap on the wrist. I finally begrudgingly reciprocated the smile to my attorney and agreed to the prosecutor's offer. I still wonder to this day if EJ would have had the courage to get on the stand and look me and my family in the eye and testify against me. Deep down I know the answer is yes, because that's what a selfish coward would do.

After pleading guilty, I had to wait nearly a month or so until I was formally sentenced. I wasn't out of the woods yet. The judge could still sentence me to the higher end of the sentencing guidelines or somewhere in the middle. As I said it was rare that a judge would go outside the guidelines, but I thought even that was a possibility with this judge, and if he did, it wouldn't be less than the guidelines. However, my attorney was reassuring me and told me that the judge would go along with the prosecutor's recommendation, since I was a low-level defendant, but nothing was in stone until I was sentenced. Either way, even if I did get the higher end of the guidelines, I knew I could do seventy-eight months in prison. I was nineteen years old and had my whole life ahead of me.

On sentencing day instead of Judge Enwright who presided over my case for the previous eight months, a visiting judge from Los Angeles, Judge Edward Rafeedie, came down to replace Judge Enwright for sentencing. During sentencing Judge Rafeedie asked me if I had anything to say before he handed down my sentence. I was too nervous to speak and deferred to my attorney, who told Judge Rafeedie that I was sorry for my actions and would do whatever I needed to do to rehabilitate myself and change my life. Judge Rafeedie said he hoped I was sincere, wished me good luck, and agreed to the lower end of the sentencing guidelines of sixty-three months in federal prison.

Unfortunately, when I was indicted, Congress had recently replaced parole with something called supervised release—therefore eliminating any opportunity of being released early on parole, so I knew the earliest release date for me was sometime in 1993, which included being eligible for fifty-four days per year good time, which would be deducted from my sentence if I earned it. Basically if I earned all of my good time, I would serve 85 percent of my sixty-three-month sentence.

Even though I had been in MCC for eight months I was terrified about the thought of going to prison. MCC had been eight months of hell of being locked away in a tall office building with no fresh air except once a week when they allowed us to go to the roof for some recreation for a few hours. Other than that trip to the roof once a week, an inmate was confined to his floor and locked in a really small cell with an even smaller window which you had to strain your eyes just to see clearly out of. I had a lot of trepidation about going to prison for the first time, but I couldn't wait to leave MCC and really start doing my time.

Fed up!

IF ANYONE EVER tells you that they were not scared the first time they went to prison, you just heard a lie. I don't care how tough one is or how tough one thinks he or she is when you go to prison for the first time you will be nervous and maybe even terrified. No matter what your street rep was before you got to prison, there is always someone there who is at least as bad as you. When you get to prison for the first time you realize very quickly you're not as tough as you thought you were. I've been told by some of the hardest gang members that even they were nervous the first and even the second or third time they went to prison. I was from the streets and had been to juvenile hall and jail a number of times for a few days, but the closest I had been to prison was my eight-month stay at MCC, and even that wasn't prison.

I got to the Federal Correctional Institution Phoenix (F. C. I. Phoenix) sometime in August 1989. If you thought going to prison was hell in itself, imagine being sent to prison in Phoenix, Arizona, for the first time at nineteen years old in the hot summer month of August. I had eight months of incarceration already under my belt, and most of my friends I grew up with had been in and out of jail and prison, so I was already aware of some prison etiquette.

Unlike state prison, particularly California state prisons, the gang and racial politics weren't as profound in federal prison, though it still very much existed. I would get my lesson on prison racial politics soon after arriving to prison. During chow I got my tray and went to sit down at an open table where no one was sitting. The table was next to a table with all black inmates eating, so I figured it was cool to sit there. As I started eating, a black inmate sitting at the table next to me who I knew had already been in prison for nine years told me to come to their table. He told me he didn't want any issues, and the table where I was sitting belonged to some big white dude who was some shot caller. I never sat at that particular table again. I learned where I could sit on that day. The guy who told me to change tables wasn't afraid and neither was I. It was just prison politics and had nothing to do with fear but everything to do with respect. In prison respect was almost as important as having enough water to drink.

There are a lot of differences between doing fed time and doing state prison time, particularly the kind of inmates who are indicted by the feds versus the numerous state crimes, but just like state prison, you have to align yourself with a group, usually along racial lines. Another difference between federal prison and state prison, in addition to aligning yourself with your race, you also align yourself with those who are from your geographical location, since you are sent to facilities all over the country. For instance, since I was black and from Southern California, I primarily associated with people from San Diego and Los Angeles.

The majority of those I automatically cliqued with were gang members and a mixture of Crips and Bloods. Because inmates in federal prison who are from California can get sent far away from home, even to the opposite coast, Crips and Bloods, at that time mostly from California, usually put their differences aside and come together under one California umbrella. Of course there was the occasional tit for tat or riot between Crips and Bloods, but for the most part because we had almost every other group of people outside of California hating us, the Southern California blacks generally stuck together. In the feds Southern California was usually considered from Fresno down to San Diego, and everything in between. Although there were guys from Oakland and other parts of the Bay Area in the feds, they had so much Bay Area pride that they would represent Oakland first then California second. That mentality usually conflicted with a lot of us from Southern California because we usually put our allegiance to California first unless there was some Crip and Blood issue.

Before I went to prison I used to hear about how federal prison was for big-time offenders. Most of the people I knew growing up went to the California Youth Authority or state prison. If someone went to the feds it was something considered major, such as bank robbery. Usually the only time we heard about federal prison was when the discussion was about the mafia, some white-collar crime, or some major drug lord. That changed in the late 1980s when Congress passed the minimum mandatory drug sentencing laws that focused attention on the inner cities across America. Around 1987 and at least ten years after, federal prosecutors sent more young African Americans to federal prison than any other group of people.* The days of federal prison being considered a white-collar or mafia prison institution were over. Federal prisons were now inundated with young black men in their late teens and twenties, many of them gang members from Southern California.

Although I was aware of the infamous reputation of federal prison, initially I wasn't too impressed. I knew I was in there with some people who were very heavy hitters while they were on the streets, but I wasn't star struck or anything. Well, I take that back. Although I never asked anyone for an autograph, there were a few times I was in awe about who I was doing time with, such as watching New York's former mafia boss John Gotti's brother Gene sweep the floor in the weight room. John Gotti was a major figure, and a lot of us young wannabe gangsters idolized him in the late 1980s, so it was definitely an awe-inspired experience for me to be right there with his brother.

It had become normal to see and talk daily with Colombian drug lords or mafia bosses, many of them not household names to the general public but very well known to the underworld. Sometimes standing in the chow line waiting to eat you would hear someone in front of you tell the person in front of him, "You know who that is? That is so and so," or "That was the guy who was on *60 Minutes*." There was no shortage of famous or infamous criminals in the feds, and it didn't take long for me to understand that federal prison really was for the big time, and I was right in the middle of it.

For me the first couple of years in prison were polar opposites of what a model prisoner's time would be like. I was still young, impressionable, and felt like I had to prove myself and hold my own. After I spent so many years of living a life of a gang member and a hustler on the street, the prison mentality in a lot of ways was just a continuation of where the streets left off. The focus for me during the first couple of years was to represent my race, represent my city and my state, and of course represent my gang affiliation. I won't say I easily adapted to prison, but being from the streets made the adjustment a little bit easier. I had it hard most of my life, so prison couldn't break me.

My prison experience was definitely not what I had visualized when I was growing up. I grew up hearing about all of the gladiator war stories in California state prisons such as Folsom, San Quentin, Soledad, and Tracy, among others. Although I had my fair share of fights while in prison and experienced several riots and near riots, being in federal prison gave me the opportunity to be around a lot of people who had been successful before coming to prison, mostly in a white-collar-related field. Of course there are people in state prison who had very successful careers on the streets, but there is no comparison to federal prison. Initially I was busy trying to prove myself as someone who was a hardcore gangsta. Eventually I would settle down, wise up, become a sponge, and soak up whatever I could from those who could teach me about life outside the prison walls.

It took about a year or so for me to adapt to my environment in prison. I wasn't becoming institutionalized or anything, but I was learning how to do my time without being preoccupied with what was going on outside of prison. I was fortunate not to be in the worst possible prison environment such as in a maximum security, so I had more time to relax and think. The hardest part of prison for me was being so far away from home and rarely receiving visits from my family. Because there were federal prisons all over the country, the Bureau of Prisons didn't make any effort to place inmates close to their homes. At first I was okay with being sent to Arizona during my first year or so. It wasn't too far from San Diego. Cynthia and I weren't a couple anymore anyway, so I wasn't expecting her to make the trip to see me often. The distance from home didn't become a big issue for me until I was sent to a prison in Lexington, Kentucky, and subsequently found out that my mother was dying from cancer.

My mother found out she had cancer while I was still in Arizona, but she would not allow anyone to tell me. It wasn't until months later while in prison in Kentucky and after having a conversation with Cynthia about how I was angry at my mother about something that she revealed to me that my mother was diagnosed with terminal cancer and the doctors had given her only a year to live. Talk about being heartbroken! I don't think I ever cried that hard in my life—definitely not in prison or around any inmates. I didn't hold back any emotion when I found out my mother was dying. I told my friends in prison, and some of them cried with me. We may have been convicts and thought we were gangsta, and some of us really were gangsta, but we could all relate to the relationship between a mother and her baby boy.

During the time of my mother's illness she was too ill to travel a long distance. I made every attempt to convince the Bureau of Prisons to temporarily send me to a prison closer to San Diego so my mother could visit me before she died. There was no way she could fly all the way from San Diego to Kentucky, even if we had the money for the trip. She was too weak and not able to make the trip.

I continued to put in requests to the prison to be relocated close to home, even if it was only temporary, and I was denied each time. My family even had my mother's oncologist send the prison a letter accompanied with medical records describing her condition. The prison's reason for not granting my transfer was that I had several disciplinary write-ups in my file. Basically the prison was saying that because I had gotten into some fights and had several verbal confrontations with staff, I could not say good-bye to my dying mother. Although I wasn't a model prisoner and understood I was in prison for breaking the law and had to accept the consequences, I wasn't in prison for some heinous crime, and I was still human. I wasn't asking for a furlough or to be set free to see my mother, I only wanted to be sent to another prison temporarily and close enough to see my mother before she died. I was never granted the transfer or able to tell my mother good-bye in person.

During my entire time in prison I was the most stressed while my mother was dying, including those early days at MCC prior to being sentenced and not knowing how much time I would receive. My faith in God was being tested like never before. Every single day before I got out of my bunk in the morning I prayed that I would keep my composure and not get into a confrontation that would cause me to lose my cool. During this time it was very precarious for me, and losing my mother made me feel like I had nothing to lose. I had always been a mama's boy, and the thought of losing her forever was becoming unbearable, and it hurt even more because I couldn't see her before she passed. Although I had felt enormous guilt for some of things I put my mother through when I was a teenager and young adult, her dying without being able to see her baby boy because of my actions made me feel like I really let her down.

A week before my mother died I had a chance to talk to her over the telephone and make my peace. I told her that I loved her and that I was sorry for all of the things I had done. I told her I knew she had done her best and that I appreciated her.

My mother succumbed to colon cancer on September 22, 1990. What I thought was an additional slap in the face, when my mother died, the prison offered to allow me to go to her funeral on the condition I pay the expense of being chaperoned by two armed US Marshals from Lexington, Kentucky, to San Diego, California. The expense included three round-trip plane tickets for the two marshals and me and hotel accommodations for all three of us, as well as the cost of ground transportation and meals during the trip. If I could have afforded the trip to my mother's funeral, I wouldn't have gone anyway. I wanted to see her and hold her while she was still alive. At this point what was the purpose? I declined the prison's pathetic offer and chose to remember my mother as the woman I last saw as beautiful, vibrant, and full of life.

There may be some people reading this who might think I don't deserve any pity for the prison refusing my requests to be at a facility closer to my dying mother. I had in fact committed a crime that caused me to be sent to prison, and it was not the prison's responsibility to make my life convenient in any way. It's true I had committed a serious crime, and I didn't blame anyone for my circumstances except myself. All I was asking the Bureau of Prisons to do was show some compassion and humanity. If it weren't for my faith in God, my bitterness after my mother passed could have destroyed my spirit and my will to survive and move forward. I own my past.

CHAPTER **16**

Times Making a Change

AFTER BEING IN prison for more than three years and serving time at six different federal prisons, I started to think about my sentence eventually coming to an end. I was a hardhead from the time I first got to MCC and throughout. I had a little less than five years total of my sentence to spend behind bars, but because of my mentality I honestly believed I could have easily turned that five-year sentence into life. However, I was surviving and soon enough would be going home and knew I had to start seriously thinking about my future.

One thing I realized early on while in prison was that being a high school dropout and not having any solid career objective would like- ly lead me back to a life of crime and a return to prison. I had recently promised myself that I would never come back to prison, but until now I hadn't come up with a plan to ensure that I could keep that promise. I was from the streets and that's all I knew. Although I had rubbed elbows with a lot of smart, educated, and successful people while I was in prison, the mentality I had of a gang member was not going to change overnight. I had spent a significant amount of time during those first few years of prison trying to live up to a reputation that I thought all young Southern California gang members had to maintain while in prison. However, I finally was beginning to under- stand how important an education could be for my success outside in the free world, so I immersed myself in every educational opportunity available that I found interesting.

The days of prisons offering significant educational programs to inmates were all but over. Congress and many state legislators had started making significant cuts to educational programs for inmates because of the public outcry that inmates were receiving too many benefits and that they should sit in prison and be punished. This outcry resulted in tough crime laws in the 1980s and 1990s, affected funding for prisons, and all but eliminated most educational opportunities for rehabilitation purposes for inmates in most prisons, even though there were studies and statistics showing that inmates who earn their GED and or other forms of higher education while behind bars* were significantly more likely not to be repeat offenders.

Visceral reaction to crime by the public and legislatures would only exacerbate recidivism; however, I didn't wait for the prison to offer me any educational opportunity. I started to educate myself by becoming an avid reader of nonfiction books. I was particularly interested in biographies and autobiographies. I wasn't particularly interested in stories about those who were great just because of who they were, but I enjoyed reading about people who had overcome adversity and went on to do something great. I admired people who had done something in spite of who they were. Reading definitely gave me an escape from my surroundings and allowed me to dream beyond the prison walls.

My first formal class while in prison was preparing for the GED test. Any inmate who did not possess a high school diploma was automatically eligible to enroll in a GED class. Not only had I dropped out of high school in the twelfth grade, but I was so busy running the streets and selling drugs at the time I barely even went to school during my last year before dropping out. Although I would like to believe I had always displayed above-average intelligence, school had never been easy for me. For various reasons I had hated school since elementary, so not surprisingly I was somewhat intimidated at the idea of going to class every day and cramming for a test on subjects I should have learned about over four years of high school. It took a little more than a couple of months of going to class five days a week before I felt that I was adequately prepared to sit for the GED exam. The idea of passing the GED may seem like a very easy task, and if I had been even a mediocre student in high school, I'm sure it would have been easy for me. Even though I treated it like a daunting task, I sat for the GED exam and passed with flying colors. I was a little irritated at myself after I got my results back, because I did a lot better than I thought and wasted a lot of precious time worrying. Putting the GED behind me was just one of several things that would be my impetus of pursuing a higher education.

During my last year or so in prison, learning had become a passion of mine. I enrolled in just about any class the prison offered. I took computer classes, real estate classes, and business classes, and if the prison had offered basket weaving, I probably would have taken that as well. Even though I still had to contend with prison politics and I remained close to my California gang associates, I was increasingly becoming an undercover nerd. Soon, however, my bookish ways became more conspicuous as I attended more and more classes. I didn't care what people thought about me. Unlike during my previous years in prison when my loyalty was to my race and California, I was now concerned for myself.

I began having a deep desire to change and become successful once I got out. Even my associations started to change during this time period while I was in prison. It wasn't like I started hanging out with prison nerds, but I started gravitating toward those who had a more positive attitude and outlook on life inside and especially outside the prison walls. It didn't matter their age or race, I just wanted to be around people who could offer me something more than the typical prison garbage that didn't do anything but breed negativity. I wanted to be around those who were focusing on their future outside of prison, people who had been successful before they were incarcerated or who aspired to be successful when they were released. I didn't suddenly become a model prisoner, but I was making a positive change and preparing myself for my impending release from prison.

With all of the disciplinary write-ups I had over the years while in prison, some arising from one-on-one fights, participation in riots, disobeying an order by a correctional office, etc., I never thought I would ever make it to the revered and much sought-out prison camp. Prison camps were generally for those who had fewer than ten years remaining on their sentence and low-level, minimum security prisoners with no violent history. Prison camps were rumored to be like country clubs. In fact prison camps were what started most of the public outrage about federal prisons and inmates living better in there than working-class people on the streets. Of course it was all a myth, but the prison camps definitely had a lot more luxuries and privileges than merely being behind a wall or fence.

Prior to the new federal drug sentencing laws, prison camps were mostly occupied by inmates who were once prominent people in their community, typically former judges, politicians, or the occasional celebrity. There was some truth to the rumors that certain federal prisons had tennis courts, swimming pools, cable television, and all kinds of other country club accommodations, but most of those privileges were stopped by the time I got there in the late 1980s. The days of club fed, although exaggerated when they existed, were long gone, even though the public perception was that prison inmates were living better than most civilians. It couldn't have been further from the truth. At one time federal prison camps were considered country clubs, and an option to make it to one after years in a high-level prison institution was an option worth pursuing.

After I went six or seven months without any disciplinary actions, achieved my GED, earned a handful of vocational certificates from all the classes I had taken, and displayed overall good behavior, which was a transformation from who I once was, I decided to ask my counselor for a transfer to a prison camp in California. I was at that time in Texas and at the seventh prison I had been sent to since my incarceration. It wasn't my first time in Texas. I had been sent to a prison about two years before in Big Springs.

I wasn't what you would call a saint while I was at Big Springs and the prison guards likely considered me as well as most people from Southern California trouble makers. One day an issue broke out on the yard between a couple of Crips and Bloods and the prison used it as an excuse to purge a number of black gang members from Southern California, because they were afraid of a major riot breaking out.

I was present, as well as almost everyone else from California, when the confrontation occurred on the yard between Lil B-Hogg from Lil Africa Piru and Big E from Lincoln Park Bloods, both from San Diego, against two Crips from L.A., Big Ken Dog from 99 Mafia Watts Crips and Lil D from 111 Neighborhood Crips. Normally everyone from California stuck together or at the least coexisted and rode together, but Lil D had supposedly been disrespecting Lil B-Hogg on some gangbanging shit and that led to a near riot on the yard. I wasn't one of the active participants in this mess, but because of my reputation and any excuse for the prison to ship anyone out from California, about a week later, I, and along with about twenty other people from California, were all shipped out to various prisons. I was shipped to Oklahoma to El Reno Federal Correctional Institution. I ended up staying in El Reno until my security level dropped from medium to minimum security, and then I was shipped back to Texas to Seagoville Federal Correctional Institution.

I had received only one visit since being in Texas, including my time at Big Springs before going to Oklahoma. In fact, I may have had three visits in three years, so I desperately wanted not only to go to a facility in California so I could have regular visits, but also, if at all possible, I wanted to go to a prestigious prison camp.

It was a long shot that my transfer request to another higher security facility would be accepted, but going to a prison camp was likely out of the question. It hadn't been that long since I was denied a temporary transfer to a high-level prison to see my dying mother, so certainly the Bureau of Prisons wouldn't allow me to go to a low-security camp in California. I had gone months with no disciplinary problems, but I still wasn't what you would call a model prisoner, but I had nothing to lose. All the prison could say was no. It wouldn't be the first time it denied me for something, and I knew it wouldn't be the last, so I made up my mind that I was going to ask my counselor if he would put me in for a transfer to Lompoc Prison Camp in California.

When I first told the other inmates from California that I had planned to put in a request for a transfer to a camp, all of them pretty much laughed at me. Most of us were in the same boat. We were gang members from either San Diego or Los Angeles, and we stayed in trouble most of the time we were in prison. We had brought our gang mentality to prison with us, and because most inmates from other parts of the country hated California people the most, we constantly had disciplinary issues. My comrades knew I had almost no chance of having my request approved and so did I. To them, getting a transfer approved to another facility was one thing, but a transfer to a camp was dreaming.

My friends were so sure my transfer to a prison camp wouldn't be approved that I even had a bet going with one of them named Arnelle. Arnelle would hook me up with one of his girls if I got accepted to a prison camp. Arnelle was a baller from Inglewood Family Bloods out of Inglewood, California, and after doing almost five years, he was one of the few cats from California who still had a lot of money and beautiful women. He knew I had enjoyed looking at his photo album and always drooled over the women in it, so even though I knew it was a long shot that my transfer would be approved, the bet gave me more initiative to fight a little harder to make it happen.

My prison counselor, Mr. Dotts, who I had always thought was aloof but nonetheless a fair man, didn't hesitate to agree to submit my request for a transfer to a camp in California. I thought he would either say no or at least agree to ask for a transfer to another higher level prison in California, but not a camp. I admit I was shocked how quickly he said yes. He was my counselor and had the authority to look at my record and see all of the write-ups I had over the years and then refuse to even submit my request. If he had done that, then I would have had to go over his head with my request to the actual Bureau of Prisons headquarters in Washington, D.C., where all the final decisions were made. By the time I would hear back from them, my sentence would have practically been over, plus that's where the decision was made to deny me to see my mother before she died, so I stood a better chance at having Mr. Dotts send it off with his endorsement.

Even though I had stayed out of trouble and vigorously pursued an education over the previous year or so, I still hadn't proven I had become a model prisoner. Nonetheless Mr. Dotts agreed to submit the request to the Bureau of Prisons for my transfer. He knew it was a long shot and told me so, but what I appreciated about Mr. Dotts was that he didn't care how much of a long shot it was. He just told me, "We'll just wait and see what happens." He probably knew it was futile but wanted to say he at least gave it a try. I'm sure he recognized my efforts to rehabilitate myself, so maybe this was his way of rewarding me for staying out of trouble and not being as much of a pain in the ass as I had been in the past.

DON'T LET YOUR PAST HOLD YOU BACK

It took about a month or so to hear back from the Bureau of Prisons regarding my transfer request. I had actually accepted the likely outcome of being denied even before I asked Mr. Dotts for the transfer, but one thing I realized around this time and that would stay with me and help me achieve some wonderful things later in my life , if I didn't try, I'd never know if I can.

I'd never forget that day sitting in the TV room watching *Video Soul* on Black Entertainment Television (BET), when I heard my name being called over the speaker to see Mr. Dotts in his office. Although I had been anticipating a response almost every day, on this particular day I wasn't thinking about it. As I walked into Mr. Dotts office nervous as hell, I could barely open his office door and walk in before he blurted out, "Mr. Bowens, they approved your transfer."

It was a surreal moment for me. This hardheaded former knucklehead was on his way, after four years, to California and a camp. To most people this probably doesn't sound like a big deal—so what? I got accepted to a prison camp in California. For me, it felt like I was a C student who just got accepted to Harvard. After so many years away from home and rarely receiving any visits, I would not only be back in California, but I would also be at a low-level security institution with a lot of the perks that came with it. My friend Arnelle never hooked me up with one of his women, but I did have a few weeks before I was transferred to the camp in California to gloat to all of my California buddies, including Arnelle.

Southern California reppin' on the federal yard FCI Seagoville

CHAPTER 17

Club Fed

AFTER A NUMBER of years in medium and minimum security prisons, I finally made it to a prison camp. Prison for me to that point hadn't been what I visualized it would be while I was growing up. I grew up believing that one day I would go to gladiator school and be in nonstop race riots and experiencing daily stabbings. Instead of going to one of the notorious state prisons that most of my OG homies went to, such as Folsom or San Quentin, my first time going to prison was to the feds. Being a federal nigga, as we call it, had a different mentality than most state prison mentalities. Yes you still have the gang and racial tension, but because of the types of crimes that send people to the feds, the caliber of inmate on average in federal prison almost forced you to think bigger than you were, even if you were a small fry on the streets. I had learned this fact as far back as my days at MCC and continued to experience it being surrounded by a number of mafia members, gang lords, and drug kingpins. But at Camp Fed I would be exposed to things and educated in ways that would change my life dramatically for the better.

Initially at the prison camp in Lompoc I was just trying to get settled in and get used to the lax atmosphere. There were no prison towers or double or triple barbwire fences. It was a strange feeling. In fact, the camp had no prison yard at all, and the inmates had the liberty to walk all over the entire facility, even when it was dark. We had access to all of the outside area when we weren't limited to lockdown hours for the night. There was a forbidden invisible line around the prison that all inmates knew not to cross or they would be considered an escapee, but as long as you stayed within or near the designated areas, you were fine. Although prison guards patrolled the perimeter intermittently, if you really wanted to just walk away, you could. People did it all the time. There were no tennis courts, swimming pools, or golf courses, but it did feel like camp fed in comparison to the other prisons where I had been. Although I was taking it all in and appreciating the moment that I had earned, the camp felt a little too mellow for me initially. I had been to several mostly medium- to high-level or medium- or minimum-level prisons, but the camp was the lowest level of minimum security. There were rarely any fights or normal tension you would expect from being in prison. Although the camp was still prison and I had to conduct myself a certain way, I knew I was in a different world when I could just walk away if I wanted to.

The camp was set up like military barracks, and inmates slept in one of two huge dorm areas with living arrangements sectioned off in cubicles. Each cubicle had two beds we called bunks, and the person you shared your cubicle with was called your bunkie. Each inmate had his own locker within his cubicle. My bunkie was a former drug dealer from Los Angeles named Star. Star had been in prison for about six years on a drug conspiracy case out of Los Angeles and he still had a couple of years left on his sentence. Star was already at the camp when I got there and had been there for almost a year. I had already known Star from another prison a few years earlier and we were already acquaintances, so it was like a reunion for us. Even though Star came from the same walk of life I did and participated in the same stereotypical activities of an inner-city youth or young adult, he had always been smarter and more positive and business-minded than most of the other people I socialized with while in prison. Particularly because of where my thought process was, it was good to

143

bunk with someone who was positive, had ambition, and could rub some of it off on me.

When I got to the camp, Star was attending a professional speaking and sales training class twice a week offered by a fellow inmate named Ben. Star attended Ben's sales training class on Saturday mornings and then attended the public speaking class on Tuesday nights. Although I was interested in doing whatever I could to receive whatever kind of education I could to put myself in a better position to be prepared to do well once I was released from prison, sales training and public speaking initially didn't sound interesting to me. I had sold a lot of drugs and was pretty successful at it, but drugs were the only product I had ever even thought about selling. Additionally I was always shy, contrary to my reputation on the street, and I hated speaking in front of groups of people I didn't know personally. The thought of attending and participating in a public speaking class was definitely not appealing to me. Nonetheless, every time Star got ready for his classes he tried to encourage me to go with him. "Come on, Lamontt, just go this one time and see what you get out of it."

Each time Star asked me to go to a sales or public speaking class with him I would give him a look that said, "Man, you must be crazy. I ain't going to those classes with all those old white dudes." Even though I was determined to change my way of thinking and my actions in particular in order to be successful when I got out of prison, I didn't think I could get anything out of public speaking and sales training.

When Star returned from his classes he would always tell me about something positive that happened and encourage me to attend next time. The classes definitely started to sound more interesting. I would see Ben around the camp and became even more intrigued by the well-polished, distinguished-looking man. Ben was only fifty years old, his hair was completely white and he had a full white beard. He looked similar to Colonel Sanders of KFC but a lot younger.

About a month or so after I got to the camp, coupled with my own interest and Star's badgering, I finally decided to attend one of Ben's Saturday morning sales training classes. The class was somewhat what I had expected. I think Star and I were the only African Americans in attendance, and most of the students were older than us. I recognized a number of the people in class from around the prison. Many of them I knew were former lawyers, doctors, politicians, and business executives, among many other former professionals whose malfeasance got them sent to prison.

Leading up to my first time going to class that morning I wasn't expecting much and had already decided it would likely be my first and last. Life is a trip, however, and it definitely had been for me up to that point, so I had no clue the effect that class would have on me and that I would come out of there a changed young man.

When class was over Star introduced me to Ben. I admit I was eager to meet Colonel Sanders. When Star and I walked up to Ben my thought was that I was going to meet some stuffy and pompous old white guy. Although Ben had never personally said or done anything to make me think he was not approachable, the perception I always had of him and the experiences I had with successful older white men, including many of those who looked like Ben, was not particular good. I was from the hardcore streets and lived the street life in the inner city. Guys like Ben were from a different world and could never relate to me, and I thought they never even tried. However, Ben and I were both inmates on relatively equal footing in Lompoc Federal Prison. He carried himself like he was bigger than that place and had an air about himself that I admit was intimidating and alluring.

During my nearly five years in prison I had come across all kinds of inmates from all walks of life, some experiences memorable, others not. Some men I admired, and others I would like to forget about, but

145

no one would have as much of a lasting positive impact on my life as Ben.

Once I got to know Ben I learned that he was a fiscally conservative Republican who grew up on a country club outside of Atlanta in the 1960s. He had been a corporate executive and top salesman, a published author, and a nationally known professional public speaker. It would be an understatement to say that Ben and I were from totally different walks of life.

Ben had run several multimillion-dollar corporations before coming to prison and I had been a crack dealer who was a multi-thousandaire from the hood. We had come from different worlds, and besides having prison in common, even in Lompoc prison we were still living in two different worlds. Ben had primarily socialized with mostly white well-educated white-collar inmates. On the other hand, I tended to socialize with mostly black inmates who were former drug dealers and former or current gang members. Nonetheless, even with our differences, Ben and I developed a friendship over the months and he would become my mentor and confidant—like a father figure.

After my initial Saturday morning attendance, I began attending both of Ben's classes regularly. I quickly realized that most of those who attended the classes and participated were well educated and already pretty good at public speaking. Most of my everyday language had been slang or Ebonics. I wasn't too intimidated, however, because my initial goal was to sit there, listen, and observe. That's exactly what I did for at least the first few times I attended the classes. There was no mandatory rule about participation. If you didn't participate you weren't getting much out of it. I was determined to better myself, which meant I would have to come out of my shell and take some chances, even if it meant being embarrassed.

The first time I got up to speak in front of the class was during the public speaking class's impromptu speech time. This was when Ben or one of his classroom assistants would give you a topic on the spot and you had a couple of minutes to think about it and then get up and speak on it for a few minutes. The public speaking class was modeled after Toastmasters, the national public speaking organization that's been around for decades. The focus in Ben's class was selling oneself through good public speaking. Ben had been a very successful salesperson throughout his career and taught us that selling yourself could enable you to sell any product or service you desired.

Most of the people who got up and spoke prior to me were pretty good speakers. I didn't speak the King's English very well. I had barely gone to school after the tenth grade, and most of the people I encountered on a daily basis spoke the way I spoke, so proper grammar and word enunciation were never things I thought about much until Ben's public speaking and sales training classes at Lompoc Prison.

Prior to my first speech I was extremely nervous. I didn't care about the overeducated white men looking at me or down on me. They meant nothing to me. I definitely wanted to impress Ben, my respect and affinity for him was growing more each day. I also was my worst critic and wanted to do well even though I lacked self-confidence. I can't recall how many people went before me, but I do recall there was more than one, and I thought they all knocked it out the park.

After each impromptu presentation, Ben and his panel of maybe two or three members of the class would critique each speech in front of the entire class. After listening to each speech before I had a chance to give mine, I almost talked myself out of it. I thought there was no way I was going to allow mostly strangers, some of whom I even thought of as snooty, judge me. I thought I could just say, "I'm not speaking" and never come back. Although Ben and I were becoming friends, I could still live with disappointing him, but deep inside I knew I had to at least give it a try. Failure was an option, but failing to try wasn't. I had to take some risks and change who I was, and if I truly wanted to move forward, I had to not only think outside the box, I would have to take myself out of the box that had been my immediate world.

I knew the clock was ticking and it would be my time to speak within minutes. I sat there nervously in an imaginary deluge of sweat pouring down my face, trying not to have a panic attack before my time was called to stand up and speak.

What I had liked most about the class was the emphasis on selling yourself, not necessarily any product or service. Both classes focused on the individual person. If the person comes across as affable and trustworthy, then the sale was almost complete and half the battle was done. Ben was a sales guru. The classes also taught how to be a better person, which in turn would open up opportunities unrelated to public speaking or selling a product or service. I had already committed myself to self-improvement and becoming a better person before I got to Lompoc prison camp, and the few classes I had attended to that point, coupled with my personal conversations with Ben and others in the class, were teaching me how to sell the good qualities about myself that would in turn help open doors for me in the future.

I don't recall who introduced me to speak, but when my time came, I got up and gave what would be the first of many speeches that I would give. Funny thing is I don't even remember the topic of my first impromptu speech or how I did. I may have even bombed, but it was a great feeling nonetheless, once it was over. I had the courage to stand up and speak and there was no turning back. It was another major step in making the transition from who I was to who I wanted to become.

The anticipation of my first major speech was no less terrifying for me than my first time getting up for my impromptu speech. In fact my major speech was a little more frightening because it was a topic I had to come up with on my own. I had an entire week to prepare for it. I had survived an initial impromptu speech without running out of the classroom or fainting, but I still wasn't an articulate and confident speaker. I still lacked a lot of the confidence I needed to speak one-on-one with some people in a private setting. I had given a few impromptu speeches and felt that my confidence as a speaker was improving, but not necessarily my skill. Those were impromptu speeches on topics we had no idea we were going to be speaking on prior to actually speaking, so unless one was a great speaker in the first place, no one was expected to knock it out the park. However, for the prepared speech, you were expected to do well because it would be on a topic of your own choosing.

The topic of my first major speech was on ancient African history. I had immersed myself in reading over the previous couple of years, and history books, particularly African and African American history books, comprised a substantial number of the books I read. In preparation for my speech I recollected what I had learned from many of those books and took notes from some of the books I still had in my possession. I decided that my speech would mention the great ancient western civilizations such as the Greeks and Romans as they are taught in kindergarten through twelfth-grade history books and used as a guide to all civilization and compare and contrast them with the ancient civilizations such as some of the great African kingdoms of Ethiopia and Egypt, among several others, that are rarely mentioned and never taught in public schools. Without trying to diminish any of the great contributions the ancient western civilizations made, I attempted to bolster many of the contributions other ancient civilizations, particularly those ancient African civilizations, made to the advancement of mankind.

It would be a passionate speech for me. I did my preparation. I thought about all of the constructive criticism and critiques I got after my impromptu speeches. I practiced, and to my astonishment, I ended up getting a standing ovation. I delivered my first prepared speech ever, and I'll never know whether the standing ovation was a courtesy, I exceeded low expectations, or I actually knocked it out the park, but what I do know is it gave me the confidence to give at least several more prepared speeches while I was in Lompoc prison. I had the confidence to co-organize and be the master of ceremony and a keynote speaker at Lompoc Federal Prisons Black History Month Celebration in 1993.

Ben would eventually take me under his wing and become one of my best friends at the camp. I continued to be close to the brothers in the prison and Ben kept his white friends, but we definitely became close, and even to this day I consider him the smartest man I've ever met.

I continued to be active in Ben's classes and became somewhat of a liaison between some of the African American inmates who were intrigued by or even critical of Ben's classes and Ben in particular. People around the prison camp who knew my history as a gang member in and outside of prison and saw my transformation were curious about the classes I had been attending. The black inmates were the most intrigued or curious, because they knew me the best and knew my reputation as not being a model prisoner. Even the prison staff inquired about me, but ironically in the most positive way. On several occasions prison staff members asked Ben how I was doing, as though they were personally invested in my progress. I had become a very active young leader at the prison camp. The skills I was gaining from my class participation and my one-on-one with Ben as well as others with similar educational and professional backgrounds would be invaluable for when I was released.

Even before I got to Lompoc and began attending the public speaking and sales training classes, I was determined to change the trajectory of my life. However, I had rarely associated with white inmates and particularly those with white-collar and professional backgrounds. I felt, and I'm sure many of them did as well, that we had nothing in common besides being inmates. I had already started associating with or mingling with a more positive group of inmates prior to arriving at the camp, but most of my friends remained black and most of them were former gang members without any former education beyond high school. At Lompoc I started associating more with the people I attended the public speaking and sales training classes with and actually became friends with some of them, with Ben becoming my best friend. My willingness to being open-minded while socializing and befriending people who were from a different walk of life allowed me to see the world outside of the limitations of the inner-city environment I had grown up in. As my confidence grew I began to see myself as more than just a former gang member and crack cocaine drug dealer. Although being a former gang member and drug dealer was and will always be a huge part of who I am and I will own it for the rest of my life, I stopped allowing those things to define me or stymie my growth to becoming something else. I began to understand that although I had been a product of my reality in my environment, I didn't have to allow it to determine my future. I own my past.

Having the opportunity to go to Lompoc prison camp after years in medium security prisons, becoming involved in the sales training and professional speaking classes, and most of all gaining a friend and mentor in Ben, was the culmination of my prison experience and would prepare me most for the subsequent struggles I would face as I strove to become the person I am today.

Me and my Dad at Lompoc Prison on visiting day 1993

CHAPTER **18**

The Big Countdown!

AFTER SERVING ALMOST five years in prison, I had been on an emotional rollercoaster. It started from my initial arrest by the US marshals while in court in January 1989 on a totally different case and then continued throughout my time at MCC in downtown San Diego for eight intensely stressful months while not knowing how much time I would eventually spend in prison and what would happen to me when I got there. I was shipped from federal prison to federal prison during a four-plus-year span and experienced some shocking things.

Early on it had become an identity battle for me. I wanted to fall back on my Christian and church upbringing for strength during the immensely challenging times, but I couldn't forget who I was and where I was. I also badly wanted to change things about me that would help me create a better life for myself, my daughter, and my son, once I was released, but again I always had to remember I was still in prison and there was never a day off from the prison politics. I was in my late teens and early twenties, some of my most impressionable and productive years. When middle-class and working-class kids would be in college, I was behind bars. Instead of going from high school to college, at nineteen years old I went straight to the University of Prison and studied at the School of Hard Knocks.

DON'T LET YOUR PAST HOLD YOU BACK

No matter how hard I tried to remain positive and dream of a better life outside the prison walls, I would have to face my reality. I was in prison. I recalled those days that I would be a gangsta nerd who took GED classes, college courses, and self-improvement classes and read vigorously and socialized with white-collar inmates. Some days I would be a straight up gangsta willing to fight, shank, or do whatever it took to prove myself, even at the risk of extending my prison stay, perhaps indefinitely. All of this had occurred in a matter of less than five years.

I had been lucky to receive only a five-year sentence in comparison to what I could have received and how much time others who were similarly charged received. By the time I got to the camp after four years I was absolutely exhausted. While growing up I always figured I would one day do something that would send me to prison for a really long time, maybe even for the rest of my life, but after sitting in federal prison for four years on a first-time conviction, I knew prison wasn't for me and the recidivism rate* need not apply.

At the time I didn't know precisely what was in my future, but I was certain prison wasn't. In retrospect, prison served its purpose in my life—good and bad.

I spent four consecutive Christmases and five consecutive birthdays locked up in federal prison. My son, Lamontt Jr., was only a month old when I was arrested in January 1989, and I had seen him only a few times after I left the Metropolitan Correctional Center in August 1989. An occasional visit from family did wonders for my psyche, and I was doing relatively well at the camp and excelling as a model prisoner with only months remaining on my sentence, but emotionally and mentally prison was wearing me down.

The countdown had officially begun when I was sentenced to sixty-three months in prison, but now I could finally see light at the end of the tunnel. Each day felt like an entire month during my final year in prison. Instead of counting down the days, it felt like I was counting down the seconds. I came to regret all the trouble I had gotten into during my previous years in prison, because now I could not use any "good time" I could have earned had I not gotten into trouble. If I had stayed out of trouble I could have earned fifty-four days off my sentence each year. Fifty-four days a year deducted from a five-year sentence may not sound like a lot, but it represented the possibility of getting out nearly 270 days earlier than scheduled. I spent my final months in the prison camp reflecting on what would have happened if I had not been a disciplinary nuisance and going to the hole* all the time. I was kicking myself at this point.

I could have been released after doing a little more than four years, but instead the earliest I would be eligible to go home would be after serving at least five years of my five-year-and-three-month sentence. I would end up serving almost my entire sixty-three-month sentence. I knew going into my last year in prison that there was no chance of me getting out of prison before late 1993.

My only hope for being released early was to get accepted to a half-way house and do the remainder of my time there. I wouldn't be completely free and I would be subject to the restrictions of the half-way house as well as under the jurisdiction of the Bureau of Prisons, but with a halfway house stay I'd at least be out of prison and back in society. I knew that the longest anyone could stay in a halfway house was six months, but the prisons rarely approved a request for such a long halfway house stay. This would especially be true for someone like me who had numerous disciplinary actions in the past.

A halfway house was for the purpose of preparing inmates for their return to society and was considered a privilege, not a right. Just like making it to the camp, I was in for an uphill battle, but I had done well during the last year and a half of my time in prison. I had been a model prisoner—at least by my own standards. I had not gone to the hole or had any disciplinary write-ups for a time and had taken enormous steps to rehabilitate myself.

Just like when I put in my request for a transfer to a prison camp in California, I knew I had nothing to lose but a lot to gain. The worst that could happen was they could tell me no. If the Bureau of Prisons denied my request to a halfway house, the worst I would face was an additional seven to eight months in prison. Either way, my time left in prison was very limited and the camp was very laidback in comparison to other prisons I had been in, but I was burnt out on prison and wanted badly to go home. It was a long shot, and for a few weeks I contemplated asking, going back and forth with whether I really wanted to go through the hassle and mental and emotional drain and getting my hopes up for something that I had no good shot at getting. However, just like putting in the request to go to the camp, I had nothing to lose, and I made up my mind and decided to ask for the maximum six months in a halfway house.

I knew I would have to dot all my i's and cross all my t's when I presented my request. Lompoc required the request for a halfway-house stay to go through your case manager and counselor before it was submitted to the Bureau of Prisons for final approval. From my recollection the bureau usually went along with the recommendation of the case manager and counselor at the prison. I was required to submit my request for a halfway house stay in writing, which I did, and then I had to wait for my counselor and case manager to respond and have an in-person meeting with me. Within a couple of days my meeting with my counselor and case manager to plead my case as to why I should be granted a halfway stay, six months at that, was scheduled. I would need to use everything Ben had taught me in his sales training and public speaking classes as well as in some of our private conversations, if I were to convince them that I should not only be granted a halfway house stay but be given the maximum six months, as well.

All I could think about was *Damn* I'm going to have to sell the hell out of myself. This was different from being sent to another prison with a lower security classification. I was trying to get released six months early. I was in for a heck of a sales pitch, but I felt I was up for the task.

On the day of my meeting with my counselor and case manager I felt pretty confident. I had made enormous strides to rehabilitate myself, and I had served a significant amount of my time. I had prayed the night before and again right before I walked into the meeting. I was prepared to articulate my argument for why I deserved a halfway house stay. I can't recall exactly what was going through my mind when I walked in that door and saw two middle-aged white men I knew to be firm but fair staring at me with a look I could only perceive as, "What is Mr. Bowens going to say to us."

Oddly I didn't feel intimidated, and they didn't come across as being judgmental or trying to make me feel uncomfortable, but I was a little nervous. My life for the next six months hinged on what those two men decided. Once I had the opportunity to plead my case, I went all the way in about how I had changed over the years and had become a better person. I went into detail about how I used to be a knucklehead prisoner, the many fights and write ups for disobeying a correctional officer's orders, which they knew from looking at my prison record, but had managed to stay out of trouble for nearly a year and a half and didn't wait around for the prison to rehabilitate me but instead rehabilitated myself. I explained to them that notwithstanding my past disciplinary actions, I was able to earn a transfer to the camp and how I accomplished numerous educational feats, including earning my GED and college credits and had become a role model at the prison camp. I looked them in their eyes with all sincerity and explained that I had proven myself to be worthy of a chance to have a head start at my new life and a halfway house would accomplish that.

I conveyed to them how much I needed the extra time in the halfway house to prepare for my transition into society. I didn't have any strong family ties in San Diego anymore like I did before I was arrested. I had lost my mother, most of my siblings were living in other parts of the country, and my son's mother Cynthia and I weren't together anymore. And although my father lived in San Diego at the time, my relationship with him and my stepmother at the time was tenuous at best. In other words, I didn't have enough strong support in the community that would ensure I would hit the ground running once I was released from prison; therefore I needed more time with my transition from prison to society, and that's what an extended time in the halfway house would offer me. I did my best to convey this information to my counselor and case manager.

The questions my counselor and case manager asked me during the meeting were typical; however I couldn't read them one way or the other and had no idea what they would eventually decide. Unlike with my previous requests to be transferred to another prison, going to the halfway house was basically the sole decision of my case manager and my counselor, with the final approval of the Bureau of Prisons. After pleading my case, leaving the meeting I still had no idea which way the men were leaning.

My case manager and counselor were gracious at the end of the meeting and shook my hand and told me they would consider my request and wished me good luck. I didn't understand why they would wish me good luck when my fate was in their hands, but nonetheless I too was gracious and appreciative of them. I left that meeting neither optimistic nor pessimistic.

About a week or so after my poignant plea for a halfway house stay, my counselor sent one of the correctional officers to my cubicle to tell me that he needed to see me in his office. I wasn't sure what it was about, but my assumption was that he and my case manager had made a decision. I instantly became anxious. I wanted to know and know right away whether or not I was going to a halfway house soon. My counselor's office was not far from my cubicle. It was probably a two- or three-minute walk, but it felt like eternity. I was going back and forth in my head asking whether they approved it or not. I didn't know how I would react either way. I needed to know, but I couldn't force myself to walk any faster, because I was so nervous. As I got to my counselor's office, the door was wide open, and he said, "I have good news for you."

I was granted a five-month halfway house stay. Even though it wasn't the full six months that I had hoped for, I was ecstatic. It usually took a few weeks for everything to be finalized before I would get my precise release date, but that didn't matter because I knew I was going to be released after being in prison for nearly five years. I would live at the halfway house in San Diego, and staying there would, I hoped, assist in with a smooth transition back into society.

Once I got to the halfway house I would be allowed to leave every day on the weekdays to look for work or go to work, and then I would return in the evening. I would have the opportunity to see my family and friends, but would still be under the authority and supervision of the federal Bureau of Prisons until my time at the halfway house had expired. Any rule violation while I was staying in the halfway house could lead to my return to prison to finish out whatever time I had remaining on my sentence.

Ben was the first person I told that my halfway house request was approved. I went straight to his cubicle and bunk and told him the good news. We went outside for a walk and talked about all the things I wanted to do once I got out and what I should expect. I knew I wanted to be a professional, but I didn't even know how to put on a tie properly. The only time I remembered ever wearing a tie was going to church as a small kid, and someone always put it on for me or I wore a clip-on, and of course we had no ties in prison. Ben and I used a belt, and he taught me how to tie a tie. I knew once I was released I would be wearing a lot of ties, so I had to learn fast how to tie them, so I continued to practice using a belt as a tie until I was released.

CHAPTER 19

Time Is Up!

I HAVE CELEBRATED every May 10 since 1993. On that day I was able to walk outside of prison a free man. I would technically still be under the supervision of the Bureau of Prisons, but I was on my way back into society after nearly five years. Although I had been ghetto rich before I got arrested in January 1989, leaving prison in May 1993, I was dead broke aside from the $200 that the prison gave me for spending money and a one-way Greyhound bus ticket back to San Diego.

The prison had given me the option of having an approved family member or friend pick me up or I could take the bus. Although I could have had someone come and get me from the prison and drive me back to San Diego, I made the choice to take the long five- or six-hour bus ride home. I thought that after so many years in prison, I could wait a few more hours to get home. Besides, it wasn't like I was about to experience some big welcome home party once I got there. I was required to report immediately to the halfway house once I made it to San Diego.

My decision for choosing to take the bus instead of the comfort of a car with family or friends was simple; I needed the extra time to reflect on and process all that I had experienced over a significant portion of my young life. I also needed to give serious thought to the challenges that lay ahead and how I would try to approach each of them. I knew my life would never be the same.

I had thoughts of the recidivism rate for those released from prison, and the odds of someone like me succeeding. My limited formal education, lack of employable skills, coupled with having only minimal family ties and financial support weighed heavily on my thoughts. Regardless of how ambitious and motivated I had become, I knew the odds were overwhelmingly against me, and on that bus, reality was sinking in fast, but I knew there was no turning back. I couldn't accept life as it once was for me, and I knew I would have to do everything within my power to never return to prison, so any fear and self-doubt I was experiencing on my bus ride home would have to be temporary.

As I sat on the Greyhound bus in the comfort of my cushioned seat looking out the window at the Pacific Ocean, I kept repeating to myself that failure was not an option. My lofty dreams had become too big for the old Lamontt. Those old dreams of becoming the biggest drug dealer were replaced with dreams of becoming a professional, a legitimate businessman, a contributing citizen to society. I also had vowed that I would be a great father to my son and that I would do everything within my power to ensure he would never end up in a gang or become a convicted felon.

The last couple of years in prison I had begun morphing into a person almost unrecognizable from the years prior. Sitting on that bus without any shackles or handcuffs, taking it all in, was more comfort and freedom than I had experienced in nearly five years. I kept thinking, praying, and meditating about the journey I had been on and the one I was about to undertake. I wasn't under any illusions, though. After all the damage I had done to my life by becoming a convicted felon of some serious crimes, succeeding against the odds would be a monumental challenge. My thoughts were all over the place as I got closer and closer to the San Diego city limits, but the more and more I realized how blessed I was to have a fresh start. Any anxiety I had on that trip lessened with every mile, and finally I would get another chance at life. However, it wouldn't take long before I realized that prison in some respects would be a walk in the park compared to what I would face on the streets as I made the adjustments to become a respectable citizen.

CHAPTER 20

A Second Chance

HAVING THE OPPORTUNITY to go to a halfway house would turn out to be an even bigger blessing than I had initially thought. I was still under the custody of the Bureau of Prisons with all the stringent rules but a thousand times better. No more double or triple barbed wire fences. No more gun towers. No more prison cells or living in a huge dormitory-style room with hundreds of other inmates. No more handcuffs or being chaperoned by a correctional officer. And best of all, no more isolation from female companionship. I hadn't experienced this feeling in so many years it took some time for me to get used to it.

The pressure to find a job was intense from the outset. To continue to be eligible to stay at the halfway house I would need to find a full-time job or at least find a part-time job and go to school. The halfway house gave its residents only a limited time to find adequate pre-approved employment. If I didn't find a job within a particular timeframe that the halfway house staff believed was reasonable, I faced going back to prison or having certain halfway house privileges taken away until I found a job.

One of the main halfway house privileges taken away, coupled with the real threat of going back to prison, was not being able to get a weekend pass to visit family and or friends. The threat of being sent back to prison usually forced most residents of the halfway house to do everything possible to find a job quickly, but in my situation it would be easier said than done. A fortunate few already had jobs lined up prior to being released from prison. I wasn't as lucky, and until I found a job, worked a full week, and paid the halfway house 25 percent of my gross from my paycheck, I would not be eligible for any weekend pass and would be confined to the halfway house unless I was looking for work Monday through Friday during regular business hours.

I had only a few items of clothing that my brothers sent me while I was in prison, but I had nothing appropriate to wear for a job interview, so I decided to take the trolley downtown to do a little shopping. I didn't have a lot of money to shop with, but I used some of the $200 the prison gave me when I was released to purchase a couple of ties, a couple of dress shirts, and a pair of slacks from the Goodwill store.

After a few days of settling in at the halfway house, I started venturing out each weekday morning in search of employment. Every week-day morning started off for me around five o'clock. Unless you were wearing ear plugs or were a deep sleeper, you would be awakened by dozens of inmates and staff walking around and talking while getting ready for work or whatever they had planned for the day. Breakfast began around six o'clock, and I started my routine by getting up, showering, getting dressed, eating my breakfast, and then signing out for the day.

I was responsible for keeping a log of every place I visited in search for employment. I was required to have someone at each location either give me a business card or sign their name with their title and provide their phone number, so I could show the halfway house proof of every place I visited. The halfway house used this information to keep a log on each residence to determine one's sincerity and effort in obtaining employment. The halfway house had an incentive for ensuring every resident had a job, and it wasn't from some altruistic concern for their residents. The halfway house earned a significant amount of money for each resident from its contract with the Bureau of Prisons, in addition to each resident paying the halfway house 25 percent of their gross income from each paycheck, so it was in the halfway house's best interest to ensure every resident had a job. Unless a resident really screwed up and violated one of the rules of the halfway house or made no earnest effort to find work, the halfway house rarely reported residents to the Bureau of Prisons. During my five-month stay in the halfway house I rarely saw anyone get sent back to prison unless there was a serious rule violation.

It took about a week before I figured out any system of looking for work. I read through the newspaper at night or in the morning look-ing for potential jobs. I clipped the advertisements or wrote down the relevant job information and then planned to visit each job to submit an application. I also just walked around downtown and other areas of the city going from business to business, even if they didn't have any *For Hire* postings. I would either submit an application for em-ployment or leave my name and number for the businesses to call me in case they had any positions available.

I didn't have a résumé, so my only means of applying for a job was submitting a job application, which many employers still allowed at the time because it was before the internet and other mass electronic communications. I didn't have a cell phone or home number, but I gave each potential employer the main number of the halfway house, and someone there would relay to me any phone messages I received.

I thought that someone who was as earnest and determined as I would find a job relatively fast during the economic boom of the mid-1990s, however, I was becoming beyond frustrated in my first month out of prison. I got up every morning and searched for gainful employment, but initially was having no luck. Every time I submitted a job application and waited for a call back for an interview, nothing. Not even getting a call for an interview to me was worse than not getting a job offer after an interview. I couldn't get anyone to even call me in for an interview. It didn't matter whether I was applying for a job as an employee of a fast-food restaurant, grocery store, car wash, or department store; I was getting no offers. I had applied to all low-level, mostly blue-collar jobs that needed no specific qualifications or experience. This was 1993 during an economic boom, not during a Great Depression or Great Recession. I filled out tons of applications without receiving one callback for an interview.

It didn't take long for me to realize at least one of the reasons for not getting any calls for an interview from at least some of the jobs. I was a convicted felon. I had to check that dreaded box each time I filled out an application. No matter how motivated I was; no matter how serious I was about turning my life around, doing right, putting my past behind me, and moving forward, I was a convicted felon and had to disclose it if I was honest. It started getting so bad for me that I thought about lying and checking the "No" box when I came across the question "Have you ever been convicted of a felony?" But I knew if I had lied and got the job, if my employer ever found out I had lied on my application, it would be grounds for immediate termination.

Talk about a Catch-22; I wanted to work, went out every single day and looked for work, but because I was a convicted felon, I couldn't work, and if I lied and said I wasn't a felon and got a job just so I wouldn't be sent back to prison, I risked being subsequently fired. In addition, if I couldn't find a job, I could get sent back to prison.

After submitting around twenty-five applications and getting no response, I stopped having any expectation of getting a call back.

I wasn't having any luck finding employment. At that point I just wanted to prove to the halfway house I was out looking for work and applying for jobs and hoped someone would give me an opportunity.

It had been almost a month, and for the first time since my release from prison, I was starting to have doubts that I would be able to turn my life around completely and become successful. With the halfway house breathing down my neck about getting employed and me adding pressure to myself about moving in the right direction, frustration was setting in.

I couldn't imagine ever going back to prison. I had visualizations of Ben with his professorial look staring at me asking, "What the hell happened, Lamontt?" At times Ben seemed to be more confident about my future success than I was. When I was feeling down or upset about something at the prison camp and I ran it across Ben, he always said, "Lamontt, you're a winner," and I started to really believe it. Although I wanted to be successful and live a good life prior to meeting Ben, at the time I didn't know what winning was. Ben, however, was certain that winning was for me, and it wasn't pumping someone's gas and definitely not being jobless. He used to tell me that if he ever saw me pumping someone's gas for money he would shoot me. I used to laugh whenever he said that. No one said it would be easy. I couldn't let Ben down. I couldn't let my mother down and believed she was looking over me from heaven. I couldn't let myself down. I had to stay focused and not give up. I had a great deal of optimism and hope upon my release from prison, but here I was after a month in the halfway house, still without a job, and struggling to find my way.

One day I decided to call my Uncle Jesse, my dad's older brother. I hadn't spoken to him since I went to prison. He and his wife, my auntie Margret, were the owners of J&M construction. He was a very successful contractor who built extravagant homes for several professional athletes, among other wealthy people. I occasionally worked for him on the weekends while I was in my teens. Uncle Jesse had become my last option, so I decided to give him a call. I didn't think to call him initially because I was definitely not trying to go into the construction business, and it had been many years since I last spoke to him and felt odd calling him out of the blue. However, I felt my back was up against the wall and I had to swallow any pride I had, so I gave my Uncle Jesse a call.

I told him my situation. He told me he would hire me immediately as a laborer. Once the halfway house cleared my employment with Uncle Jesse, he started picking me up from the halfway house every weekday morning and sign me out for the day. Every Friday he would write me a check and I would cash it and give the halfway house 25 percent of the gross amount and would be cleared to have my week-end pass either staying with my dad and stepmother or with Uncle Jesse and his family. I would return to the halfway house Sunday evening and then repeat my weekday routine beginning on Monday morning. Uncle Jesse was my guardian angel.

While I worked for Uncle Jesse he would take me to various job sites daily and then drop me off with one of his foreman for the day. After working as a laborer for a couple of weeks and the initial excitement that I had about having a job and beginning my life earning an honest living began subsiding, I knew that being in the construction business, particularly as a laborer, was not for me.

First, I couldn't hit a nail straight if my life depended on it. It was scorching hot during the summer months in San Diego, and practically all the job sites where I worked were outside with barely any shade. There was no question I was happy that I was working and extremely grateful that my uncle was providing me the opportunity to make an honest wage, coupled with the fact it allowed me to get weekend passes, but my heart wasn't in it, and Uncle Jesse recognized this fact right off the bat.

Sometimes I came back to the halfway house in the evening literally covered in dirt from head to toe and two shades darker. My uncle knew I wasn't cut out for that kind of work, and he never tried to turn me into a carpenter. Although I worked hard and appreciated every day I worked for him, my uncle told his foremen that I had no desire to become a carpenter and for them not to work me too hard and not to try to turn me into a carpenter. I was the quintessential spoiled nephew of the boss, and his foremen and other laborers resented me for it, but I didn't care how anyone felt about me or my position as the boss's nephew. I took it as a blessing and still worked hard every time I was on a jobsite. I realized it was a temporary stepping stone for me, and I was blessed to have an uncle who was willing to help me get on my feet.

I owe Uncle Jesse a lot of gratitude for everything he did for me during that time. I don't think I would be where I am today if he had not opened his heart and allowed me to secure a job when I was at one of my lowest points. He owed me nothing, and considering he really didn't need my help, he still ended up paying me every week just so I could stay out of prison and get weekend passes. I'm immensely grateful for my uncle's support.

CHAPTER 21

High Hopes

I CONTINUED TO press forward, working on various construction sites every day, but all that was about to change once I started talking to my boy Bruce and found out what he was up to. Bruce was a good friend of mine who was also a resident of the halfway house. Bruce and I had known of each other from the streets prior to going to prison, but we didn't become friends until I ran across him while I was in prison.

Before I went to prison Bruce and his boss had been suspected of robbing my boss Junior for seventy-five thousand dollars. Bruce was considered one of the main culprits. After the robbery a hit had been put on Bruce and twice he narrowly escaped with his life. Junior and Bruce's boss eventually resolved the robbery issue and became close friends.

There was never any kumbaya moment between me and Bruce until we got to prison. Our bosses had become friends but we never really interacted with each other on the streets nor did we care to. I actually became friends with his boss before Bruce and I became friends. His boss and I were in MCC together and were cellies (cellmates) for a couple of months.

DON'T LET YOUR PAST HOLD YOU BACK

I always thought it was strange how prison could bring peace between former enemies if they are the same race. Not only was I cellies with his boss, but Bruce and I had become good friends after serving time together in Texas. Unless someone killed a family member or close friend of yours, if you were the same race, nine times out of ten you would leave whatever animosity you might normally have on the street—at least that was my experience in federal prison.

And even in those rare cases when you might run across someone who had something to do with one of your homie's murder, there still might be a way to peace. My workout partner while in Seagoville FCI was OG Tattoo from 4 Tray Gangsters. Initially we didn't speak to each other for four months with people on both sides in our ears. Finally we broke the ice, talked about the streets and left it there, then became cool. Although federal prisons didn't have the same level of racial tension as the California state prisons, you still typically aligned with your race and those from your geographical area.

Bruce had gotten to the halfway house a month or so before I did. We talked daily. He was aware how desperately I wanted to get out of the scorching sun as a construction worker. He would see me come back to the halfway house in the evening covered in dirt. He also knew I had plans to work in the community with at-risk youth and someday give back with my time and other resources. One day after I got back to the halfway house, Bruce told me about an organization he was thinking about joining called Triple Crown, a nonprofit organization run by a local reverend named Ray Smith who gave felons and former gang members job opportunities. What I liked about Triple Crown was that even though most of the work was blue collar and manual labor, in the evening and on the weekends, members had an opportunity to speak to at-risk youth about the dangers of gangs and crime. I had spent the past year in Lompoc Prison planning to help at-risk and underprivileged youth once I got out, with the hopes that they wouldn't make the same mistakes I made. Triple Crown sounded exactly like the kind of organization I wanted to be associated with.

I called Uncle Jesse that night and told him he didn't have to pick me up the following morning because I was going to see about another job. I took days off occasionally either to handle miscellaneous business or look for other job opportunities. My uncle had no problem with me taking days off because not only did he know I was pursuing other career opportunities, he actually encouraged it.

The following morning Bruce and I took the trolley down to the Triple Crown office on Imperial Avenue in the heart of Southeast San Diego and met with Ray Smith, the Executive Director. After Bruce introduced me to Ray, we talked for several minutes about what his organization did and then I told him about my plans and what I wanted to get from Triple Crown—particularly reaching out to the youth. I wasn't just looking for a job to make a little money to pay for my daily necessities; I wanted to use Triple Crown as a stepping stone to a career. After our brief meeting and an informal interview process, Ray invited me to join as a member of Triple Crown.

Triple Crown received government contracts and hired workers, typically felons and others from various neighborhoods in the inner city, to work at various jobs. Most of the jobs consisted of cleaning up brush or removing old building scraps in preparation for some type of landscaping or building project. Other jobs involved removing brush for the city for aesthetic purposes only. The work was menial and the pay was minimum wage. One drawback from my time working at Triple Crown was that I got paid only if I worked. Often there weren't enough contracts or monies from contracts available for every worker, which meant those with less seniority sometimes didn't work. I didn't take the job at Triple Crown for the pay, however, because I could have done less of the same type of backbreaking work with my uncle for the same pay and more consistency in pay. What Triple

Crown offered me was community contacts and various programs and events I could participate in.

I wanted to continue to work with Triple Crown doing community outreach and activism, however I still had to pay bills and needed full-time employment, and off-and-on-work as a laborer wasn't sufficient. In the interim, however, I continued to search for more stable employment, and once I found another steady nine to five, I could still work with and support Ray and Triple Crown as a volunteer.

Finding work outside of Triple Crown remained difficult. I went on a couple of interviews but nothing materialized. Just as I was ready to give up on Triple Crown and start working with my Uncle Jesse again, Ray and a prominent local attorney by the name of Mike Duckor, started an organization together called High Hopes.

High Hopes was a derivative organization of Triple Crown, and most of its initial members also were employees of Triple Crown. Members of High Hopes were mostly people from the community who had been incarcerated and/or had been involved in gangs at some point in their lives and were trying to turn their lives around. The huge difference between Triple Crown and High Hopes was High Hopes focused on getting its members full-time employment with reputable companies around the city, whereas Triple Crown offered only temporary and often intermittent employment doing menial jobs without any medical and dental benefits.

Triple Crown employment was good for younger people who needed immediate help with getting off the streets and getting on their feet, whereas High Hopes promised its members potential careers where they could have a sustainable life and raise a family.

Another difference between High Hopes and Triple Crown was the level of community activism. In Triple Crown we would give occasional speeches to local churches or youth groups during the evening, whereas High Hopes was a full-time community outreach organization that required its members to sit on panels, meet with various local and statewide politicians, and commit to a number of public-speaking events throughout the week. High Hopes members were also required to attend at least one meeting per week during the evening, which was usually held at Mike's law office. And unlike Triple Crown, which would hire almost anyone who could at least perform the menial work, High Hopes was much more selective in its membership. High Hopes mission was for its members to be gainfully employed with various types of businesses. For example, Mike asked his colleagues at a number of law firms to hire at least one member of High Hopes.

High Hopes was definitely more related to what my ultimate professional plan was, and I knew from the outset when it was first formed that I wanted to be a part of. It was a unique concept in San Diego. Never before had I heard of a prominent white businessman, or, as in Mike's case, a lawyer, put his reputation on the line by helping felons and former gang members get good paying jobs with his friends and colleagues at prominent law firms and other businesses around the city. This perk was definitely why membership was more selective, and participants were required to get involved in extensive meetings and community outreach. High Hopes was an organization that helped place convicted felons and former gang members in business establishments that were not accustomed to hiring people with such backgrounds, thus the vetting process was stringent.

Ray had been in the Southeast San Diego community most of his life, and Triple Crown was accustomed to working with many felons and former and active gang members. Mike was a prominent attorney with his own successful law practice. Some of us were going to be placed in various law firms and other reputable businesses around the city and county. Ray and Mike wanted to be sure all High Hopes members were serious and up to the challenge. None of us ever worked in a white-collar environment, and most of us never even worked in any well-established business. We were from the streets and were alien to the working world we were about to enter. Those who proved that they were serious eventually got their opportunity to be employed with one of the law firms or other businesses with the hope of using it as a stepping stone to someday having a career. I didn't hesitate to let Ray and Mike know I was very interested in participating in High Hopes. I knew right off the bat that I was up to the challenge. High Hopes had been exactly the kind of thing I thought about while I was in prison during my transition phase working with Ben.

Although I had never worked in a white-collar environment, I had briefly immersed myself in a world with former attorneys, judges, businessmen, doctors, politicians, and other professionals during my last seven or eight months in Lompoc prison camp. Nevertheless, I sensed that the world I was about to enter would be completely alien to me, nothing like I've ever experienced.

CHAPTER 22

Legal Business

AFTER I HAD worked several months off and on with Triple Crown and then with the initial startup of High Hopes, Ray and Mike told me that I had an opportunity to interview for my first law-firm job. I was ecstatic. I believed all of my perseverance was beginning to pay off. Just months earlier, I had been in prison with no idea where I would find my first job, and then after being released and all the initial difficulty and frustration with finding work, who would have thought I'd be given such an opportunity?

Within months of being released from prison after serving nearly five years, without earning a high school diploma—only a GED—and as a felon for some serious crimes, I was getting an opportunity to work at a law firm. I had about a month remaining in the halfway house, and I still had to get any employment approved by the halfway house before I could accept an offer. The law firm job would be as driver for a wealthy attorney in the Del Mar area of San Diego. It didn't sound ideal, nor was it what I had expected to be my first office job, but it sounded rewarding nonetheless and it would be steady income and I would be making above minimum wage. It would also finally get me from working out in the hot sun and I would have medical benefits.

I was given the law firm's contact information and told to call to schedule an interview. From the excitement of moving forward and having potential opportunities that I had dreamt of, I don't think I was even nervous when I called to schedule the interview. I don't recall how soon the interview was scheduled after I called to set it up, but I do know I didn't want to waste any time and wanted to have it as soon as possible.

The day of the interview I borrowed my girlfriend's car and drove to the office in Del Mar. The interview was scheduled for the morning on a weekday, and it was about a forty-five minute drive in morning traffic from where the halfway house was located in Logan Heights to the office in Del Mar. The long drive gave me an opportunity to reflect on what I was about to experience, similar to what the long bus ride had done for me after I was released from prison. I remember saying repeatedly to myself, "Lamontt, you got this." Even though I hadn't gotten the job yet, I felt an immense feeling of accomplishment.

The office manager was an older woman, probably in her early to late forties. I was only twenty-three years old, and considered any-one over forty "older." She was very polite and asked me a number of questions, particularly about my criminal past, which I didn't feel uncomfortable elaborating about. She then took me around the of-fice, which was relatively small, and introduced to several people I believe may have been secretaries, and then she introduced me to the guy who was the current driver for whom I would be taking over. The current driver was the boss's nephew, and he was preparing to leave for grad school. The attorney I would be driving for, who was the head partner, wasn't in the office the day I had my interview, so I was unable to meet the person I would be directly working for. However, after the interview I was under the impression that I was hired on the spot. This had nothing to do with any outstanding interviewing skills or exceptional ability I may have had, but it had everything to do with Mr. Duckor.

Mike was a prominent and well-respected attorney. His colleagues who offered to hire one of his guys from High Hopes usually took his word that we were worthy of the opportunity. The interview was just a formality, and all I had to do was get through it without making a fool of myself or displaying any negative stereotypes of a felon, and I would get the job.

Before I could start my new job, I had to give the halfway house all the information pertaining to the job, and the directors there would then need to discuss all the particulars with my prospective employer. This was the same process I had to go through when I took the job with Uncle Jesse as well as with Triple Crown. The halfway house director or the assistant director did most of the employment approvals.

The office manager at the law firm called the halfway house to discuss my position with the assistant director. The job was as a driver in Del Mar and would sometimes require me to drive my new boss occasionally to Orange County, which was almost a two-hour drive from the halfway house.

I understood that certain jobs might conflict with my obligations to comply with the rules and regulations related to traveling and curfew restrictions of the halfway house. I was also aware of residents of the halfway house who worked the graveyard shift or who had flexible work schedules that changed periodically. If I ever needed to go to Orange County, I thought I could call the halfway house and tell them I may be working late and would return as soon as I got back to San Diego.

This job was an opportunity to finally get a fulltime job, not to mention at a reputable law firm even if it would be only as a driver. The assistant director at the halfway told the office manager I couldn't accept the job and refused to allow me to work there. I had only a month or so left in the halfway house. I was furious.

I felt there was some hating on my success by the assistant director. There was absolutely no hesitation for the assistant director to approve my prior requests to work with my uncle or with Triple Crown when the job was back-breaking construction work for minimum wage, but when I had an opportunity after being released only several months from prison and still in the halfway house to work as a private driver for a prominent attorney, it seemed she took a special interest in opposing it and sabotaged it. Of course there's a chance she had no ulterior motive for denying me the job, but I suspect there was.

After persevering through the indignation of applying to dozens of jobs and not receiving one interview, then working as a laborer with my uncle and Triple Crown, then finally getting a full-time job offer with a law firm that would provide me with full medical benefits, pay me above minimum wage, allow me to have some financial stability once I was released from the halfway house, and then to have it all taken away before I even got it, was disheartening to say the least.

Not getting the job as a driver felt like the Catch-22 situation about checking the box on a job application that asks if you have ever been convicted of a felony. Damned if you do; damned if you don't. I felt like the system once again demanded that I do well or at least well enough, but at every opportunity it made it harder for me to get ahead. I admit walking around that halfway house after that disappointment was not easy. Every time I saw the assistant director, the thoughts that went through my mind about her were not good. I tried to keep a normal expression on my face whenever I saw her, but it got to a point where I'm sure she could tell I couldn't stand her. The halfway house assistant director never even had the courage to tell me what she had told the office manager over the telephone about my not being able to take the job. I had to learn about it from the office manager herself when she rescinded the job offer and explained her reasons.

Although I was grateful for the intermittent work I was able to do with my uncle and Triple Crown, deep inside and maybe even on the surface, I knew there was so much more for me. High Hopes continued to be very rewarding for me, with all of activities we had going on in the community. I kept my head down and stayed busy until another opportunity arose, which Ray and Mike assured me would happen.

My stay at the halfway house was about to come to an end. It was hard to believe that I had been out of prison and in the halfway house for five months. In hindsight, even with the setbacks I had experienced during those five months, I really did hit the ground running when I came home from prison, because those five months flew by.

Prior to being released from prison and even up until a month or so before my time was up in the halfway house, I had no idea where I was going to live. I sometimes used my weekend passes to visit with my dad and his family, where I felt completely at home, but where I would live once I got out of the halfway house was still undetermined.

My father and I hadn't been particularly close since he and my mother divorced when I was seven years old. He had just started to come to visit me in prison when I got to Lompoc. I must say, however, even with the resentment and bitterness I had toward my dad about how everything went down when he and my mother divorced, when I came home from prison he was there for me like any good parent should be. I was twenty-three years old and I finally had the father I always needed and wanted.

Finally I had my living situation lined up once I was discharged from the halfway house. I was going to live with my father and stepmother in Southeast, ironically in the Skyline area where it all started for me when I was a kid. Obviously I couldn't afford to move out on my own, but my father had offered me my own bedroom, and there would be no pressure for me to move out until I got on my feet. He told me I could take all the time I needed to get myself together. Although I had already potentially ruined my life with gangs, drug dealing, and prison, if I had any chance of overcoming my past this was perfect timing for me to have strong family support, particularly from my dad.

That time living with my father was a blessing because not only did I really need him and my stepmother and they were really there for me, it also gave all three of us a chance to become close. I had never thought I would ever come to feel like my stepmother was a mom to me, but it eventually happened, better late than never.

I started to settle in as a regular citizen after leaving the halfway house. I had begun adjusting to living with my dad and stepmother and working with Triple Crown and High Hopes and occasionally with Uncle Jesse. It was time for me to become well acquainted with the stringent rules of my supervised release—formally called parole. I had been sentenced to five years' supervised release on top of my original sixty-three-month sentence. This aspect was just another cruel one that Congress included in its draconian "get tough on crime" laws of the 1980s targeting the crack cocaine epidemic. Not only did Congress eliminate parole and require a defendant to serve at least 85 percent of his or her sentence, but it also tagged on a minimum of three years, but most of the time five years or more, of supervised release.

For the next five years I would have to report to my probation officer on a regular basis, submit to random drug testing, and be subject to travel restrictions and random unannounced home searches, among many other things. It was kind of like double jeopardy. I was sentenced to five years in prison and served my time, but if I violated any of the terms of my supervised release, I could be sent back to prison to serve an additional five years. For all intents and purposes, I had received a ten-year sentence with five of it on parole.

For reasons I may never know, Chief Probation Officer Kelly LeBaron was assigned to my case. Out of twenty-two co-defendants, with me being number twenty-two, the powers that be assigned me to a senior probation officer. I had already heard about Mr. LeBaron's reputation as a hard-nosed probation officer who wouldn't hesitate to send a person back to prison for a probation violation, so I knew there was no room for error on my part. It was a good thing that I was determined to stay crime free and never return to prison, but I also knew that task was easier said than done when you're faced with petty probation rules coupled with a hard-nosed probation officer. I didn't know what to expect, but I was fresh out of the halfway house and ready to move forward with whatever I had to face.

When I first met Mr. LeBaron at the United States Probation Office, he came across exactly as the person I was expecting. He had a stern look on his face, and after introducing himself and shaking my hand, he went right into a litany of rules I would need to adhere to as well as his expectations of me. My first meeting with Mr. LeBaron was surprisingly brief, which was probably because he got straight to the point with no small talk. I was intimidated by this man because of his reputation, the way he came across, and the fact that my freedom was in his hands. I thought there was no way I could survive for five years with this guy breathing down my neck. I left that meeting with my probation officer for the first time not feeling good. I didn't give Mr. LeBaron much thought after a day or so leaving his office. I knew I had to call in every day to see if my number came up for a random urine sample and I was scheduled to meet him a couple times a month. Other than that, there was nothing else I had control over. I just had to follow the rules of my probation, which I had every intention of doing.

With the exception of the frightening first meeting I had with my probation office, the start of my supervised release was uneventful and fine; however, my worst thoughts of facing Mr. LeBaron for any rule violation would come a lot sooner than I ever expected. Prior to my next meeting with Mr. LeBaron, I was at home and in excruciating pain from a migraine headache. I asked my stepmother if she had anything to help me with the pain, and she gave me one of her prescription Vicodin pills. At the time I had no clue what Vicodin was or that it was considered a narcotic. I trusted my stepmother not to give me something that would physically harm me, and I knew she wouldn't intentionally do something that would get me sent back to prison, so I didn't think anything of taking the pill. I hadn't smoked any weed since prison and had no desire to use any illicit drug ever again. I rarely used drugs since my late teens, and wasn't about to start, so a prescription pill from my stepmother was the last thing I thought could get me in trouble with my probation officer and sent back to prison.

About a week after I took the Vicodin, my number came up to take a urine test. I thought nothing of it because I had done nothing wrong. It would be my third or fourth urine test since I was on supervised release and the other tests had been clean, and I thought this one would also. However, a couple days later I got a call from Mr. LeBaron telling me that I needed to come down to his office the following day.

Mr. LeBaron was already intimidating enough in person, heightened by his reputation, but to hear his voice over the telephone in such a direct way was troubling. I still wasn't particularly worried, because I had done nothing wrong and had no intentions of doing anything wrong and thought maybe he just wanted to see me on some administrative matter. I was able to sleep that night but not without some concern and tossing and turning.

The following day I went to Mr. LeBaron's office, and as soon as I walked in and sat down, he lit into me. If I recall correctly he accused me of using opioids or crystal meth; I don't remember the exact drug, but I knew I hadn't used any illegal drug, and it took me a second to realize that the positive urine test must have been caused by the Vicodin my stepmother gave me. For the first time since I had been out of prison I thought there was a strong possibility I could go back. I swore that I would beat recidivism, but at that moment I wasn't sure.

As Mr. LeBaron was threatening to send me back to prison among other consequences of a dirty urine test, I was able to explain to him that my stepmother had given me one of her prescription pills for my headache and that she had a valid prescription and I could call her and she would verify what I was telling him and we could bring the prescription to him. After I was able to give Mr. LeBaron my explanation, he calmed down. I figured what I was telling him made sense, because he seemed to accept my explanation, but I was still terrified. After my initial scare of having a "dirty" urine test and potentially being sent back to prison, Mr. LeBaron gave me a stern warning (and a scare) to be careful what substances I put into my body. The topic never came up again.

Although Mr. LeBaron initially lived up to his reputation as a no-nonsense, I'll-send-you-back-to-prison-in-a-heartbeat probation officer, I would soon learn that you can't always judge a person until you get to know the person. It would be particularly a good lesson for me in regards to any type of law enforcement official. I had been conditioned from a very young age to believe that any person in a position of authority—particularly law enforcement and especially if they were white—was my enemy and was out to get me. Oddly Mr. LeBaron not only did not send me back to prison or discipline me in any way, but over the months while he was my probation officer I also grew fond of him, and we developed a mutually respectful relationship. Although I never forgot who he was and that he was in a position of power and could send me back to prison, after that initial scare, I never again felt like he was out to get me or felt intimidated by him as though he was some villain. As long as I did my part by staying out of trouble and adhering to the rules of my supervised release, I was good, and aside from the occasional urine tests, Mr. LeBaron rarely came to check on me at my house and never came to my job. In fact after a few months I would have to call him and ask if he needed me to come down and see him, because our interactions became so infrequent it was almost like I wasn't on supervised release.

Eventually Mr. LeBaron took me off of his caseload and I was assigned to another probation officer, but I would run into him occasionally either at the probation office while seeing my new probation officer or walking on the street. We remained cordial, and many years later I ran into him and he even invited me to his retirement party.

After I had been out of the halfway house for a couple of months and was re-acclimating to life on the outside, the only thing that was still lingering and felt like it was stymieing my progress was finding steady employment. Although I was still disappointed about not being able to work at the law office as a driver in Del Mar, I would soon realize how not being able to work there may have been a huge blessing in disguise. I hadn't been thrilled about being a driver in the first place and would have preferred being indoors in an office socializing, net-working, and learning. Also I didn't own a car at the time, and taking public transportation to Del Mar all the way from either the halfway house or where I lived with my dad in Southeast would have been a pain. I was about to realize the biggest blessing in disguise from that initial disappointment.

Even with some of my setbacks and disappointments, I was sold on High Hopes and continued to be dedicated to my work with it and attend our meetings regularly. I also knew I needed to hang in there and be patient and that eventually I would get another opportunity at a job. One night at one of our meetings that's exactly what happened. Our meetings were held after work hours in a conference room in Mike's plush law firm in downtown. There were about twelve mem-bers of High Hopes, not including Mike and Ray. We would sit at the huge marble conference room table and discuss topics ranging from community activism to local and national politics. Primarily Mike and Ray wanted members to be involved in the community at every level, in addition to having a day job. I was young and on a mission to learn as much as possible and be successful, so I particularly enjoyed attending our meetings and soaked in as much as I could.

At this particularly meeting Mike and Ray informed me that I was next in line for a job interview. After losing out on the first job, I wasn't sure if I was going to have an opportunity at another law firm, even though law-firm jobs were the most prevalent because of Mike's position in the legal community, High Hopes also set up interviews for its members in other well-established fields. We had members who got electrician apprenticeships and members working in supermarket meat departments who later became butchers, for example, and others worked in other fields; however, I think early on I was sold on working in a law firm since prison. I had dreamed about becoming a professional and working in a white-collar environment. I knew I wasn't particularly good working with my hands, as evidenced by my lack of any natural ability to drive a nail, though my uncle was a prominent contractor and my dad was a jack of all trades when it came to fixing things. I was determined to be in an office, whether it be a law office, a bank, or some other corporate entity. Well maybe not a bank.

Mike told me that the potential job would be with a prominent law firm downtown and that it would be a great place for me to work and get my start. He said he would contact me in a couple of days with the details to set up an interview. I was excited just from hearing where the office was located. I still didn't have a car and was taking the trolley everywhere, and downtown was the most convenient location for me to get to and from work. My dad and stepmother had also recently moved only several blocks from the trolley line that ran right through downtown. I was excited to have another opportunity at working a nine-to-five, particularly in exactly the environment that had been my plan for a while.

A couple of days went by before I got the call from Mike with the contact information for the job. He gave me the telephone number and told me to ask for Kathi, who was the office manager. Although I was excited about the possibility of finally being gainfully employed and working in an office, especially at a law firm, I had never actually had a real office job. The few months I worked in the prison warehouse was nothing like it would be working at a medium-sized, prestigious law office, but this was exactly the opportunity I had been hoping and working for, and it was becoming a reality.

This time there were no barriers to getting my job approved before getting hired, and if I was hired, I'd just need to contact Mr. LeBaron with my new employment information. I was conscious of the fact that there was a possibility that I wouldn't get the job, but all the potential employers knew what High Hopes was, and I know Mike told the law firm all about my particular past before it agreed to grant me an interview. There would be no "checking the dreaded box here," though I might need to explain my past during the interview, and I was perfectly okay with doing that. After hearing the news from Mike and getting the office manager's contact information, I was pretty confident, and unless I bombed during the interview, there was an excellent chance I would be hired.

If I recall correctly I think I called Kathi immediately after getting off the phone with Mike. It seemed like everything took at least a couple of days to happen. I was particularly surprised that when I called Kathi she told me she could interview me the following day. Even with all my ambition and excitement, things were moving a lot faster than I expected. I wasn't expecting to get through to Kathi on my first call, but I did, and I definitely wasn't prepared for her to say she could interview me the following morning. What I would learn from this experience and continue to learn over the years is that opportunity is on its own schedule, and if you're in the game of life and trying to get ahead, you'd better be ready, because opportunity waits for no one.

That following morning I put on one of the newer suits that I had recently purchased for a little more than a hundred dollars at the Fam-Mart Indoor Swap Meet, also known as Fam-Bam. I wasn't and still am not a big fan of cologne, but that morning I also put on some cologne and made sure I was groomed. I then said a prayer and headed to the trolley station for my journey downtown. The trolley ride from where I lived to downtown with at least seven or eight stops in between probably took about thirty minutes. This ride gave me time to prepare in my head for the interview. I wasn't sure what kind of questions Kathi would ask me, but I made a conscious decision to be myself and be honest, particularly if my past came up. The closer I got to downtown the more nervous I got, and I could feel the cheap suit I was wearing become moist from my sweat. It was a late November day, warm even for San Diego, and the suit I was wearing was probably a winter suit.

Somehow I managed to exit the trolley and make it to the office building without being drenched in sweat. I was able to compose myself, and after checking in with the building security, I entered the elevator ready to enter a world that I hoped would change my life forever.

After going up eighteen floors, when I exited the elevator the first thing I saw was an enormous fish tank built into the wall with numerous exotic fishes swimming around. I thought, am I ready for this? There were two receptionists sitting next to each other who greeted me. I told them my name and that I was there to see Kathi. One of the receptionists told me to have a seat and that she would let Kathi know I was there.

Kathi came out about five minutes later and escorted me to her office.

DON'T LET YOUR PAST HOLD YOU BACK

As I was walking down the hallway to Kathi's office, I saw that most of the people were wearing jeans, shorts, T-shirts, and tennis shoes. I was dressed in a cheap, stuffy suit I had imagined most people would wear in this type of environment. That dress style was definitely not what I had envisioned for a law firm. Because of the huge built-in fish tank coupled with how everyone was dressed, saying I was taken aback would be an understatement. I guess I didn't know what to expect. The law office I had previously interviewed with in Del Mar was small and I only got to meet a few employees there who I assumed were secretaries. Our High Hopes meetings were held at night at Mike's office after most of the people left for the day. Besides working with Mike at High Hopes, my only previous contact with lawyers were my criminal defense lawyers and the former lawyers I met in prison who were also inmates. I was expecting people to walk around in business suits with briefcases, but what I got from my first impression was a plush office with a lot of beautiful people who looked like they were on their way to a picnic or baseball game. It wouldn't take long for me to realize that they were some of the smartest and most talented attorneys in the industry, regardless of how they dressed in the office.

Surprisingly I wasn't nervous anymore and felt very relaxed during the interview, even though I was still a little uncomfortable because I wasn't sure if my past would come up. Kathi was aware of my background because I wouldn't have been there, had she not. The interview probably lasted about twenty minutes or so and Kathi told me she would be in touch with me. I was aware of the fact that just because I was a part of High Hopes and Mike set up the job interview, it didn't automatically guarantee me the job. Nonetheless I left the interview feeling good about my chances.

Two days went by, and I heard nothing from Kathi. I was tempted to give her a call by the end of the second day but decided against it. On the fourth day without hearing anything from Kathi, I started to worry. I thought that maybe I didn't get the job. I reflected on my performance during the interview. Did I sell myself as Ben would say? Did I come across as genuine or likeable? I wanted the job really badly and had a gut feeling after that interview that it was the place for me. After the fifth day of not hearing anything, I decided to give Kathi a call. I needed to know one way or the other.

The receptionist put me on hold and then came back and told me Kathi was unavailable and asked if I wanted her voicemail. I left a short message asking about the status of the job and hung up. To my surprise within minutes Kathi returned my call and told me she had been meaning to contact me but she had been busy and hadn't had the chance. Our conversation was brief but not too brief for Kathi to offer me the job and ask when I could start.

Who would have thought that at the age of twenty-three, straight out the hood, and only seven months after serving five years in prison, I would land my first full-time job with a prestigious law firm? I could remember just only eight months prior hanging out at the prison camp with Ben and his buddies who were former lawyers and judges and dreaming about someday being in a white-collar setting when I got out. Now here I was, and the feeling was surreal. It was something that would have been unimaginable when I lived on the Four Corners of Death. I definitely didn't have time to dream of a better life while in the middle of gang wars in East Dago.

As horrible as prison is and my experience there was 85 percent of the time, not only did it literally save my life, but I can also honestly say if I had not gone to prison when I did, I probably would never have been in the position to get the job at Milberg Weiss. It wasn't that my bad behavior was being rewarded by getting a job at a prestigious law firm right after I got out of prison; it was about society living up to its so-called creed that we are a country of second chances. If I did my part in paying my debt to society by spending nearly five years in prison and then doing everything within my control to rehabilitate myself and change my negative behavior, I deserved my second chance, and this law firm would turn out to be the second chance of a lifetime.

Milberg Weiss was a medium-sized law firm and had a philosophy of work hard and play hard. One way management rewarded its employees for their dedication and hard work was allowing them to come to work dressed casually. This dress code was a far cry from most law firms, and it made sense, considering at Milberg rarely had any clients come into the office. The casual dress code allowed people to put their heads down and use their talents working instead of being preoccupied with an outdated culture of being stuffy with no apparent benefit to the bottom line.

My primary position with the firm was working in the fax room, but I also occasionally helped out in the mailroom and copy room. Although some might think working in the fax room should have been a less than desirable position, it was one of the proudest moments of my life, and I worked my ass off and did it well. Because of where I had come from and what I had been through, particularly over the prior five years, I was going to take advantage of this opportunity whether it was in the fax room or lunchroom or any room, and I was not going to screw it up. I was happy to have a decent job and be making an honest living, and yes, being out of the hot sun and being in an air conditioned environment was a major plus.

When I first started working in the fax room in late 1993 most people hadn't started using email, at least not to send documents. Almost every business, including law firms, was using fax machines as the primary means for sending documents electronically. I worked in a small room no bigger than a walk-in closet in a single-family home. We had about six fax machines, and all of them were working and going at the same time. My day from the time I got to work at 7:30 a.m. until the time I left at 4:30 p.m. would consist of sending and receiving faxes and delivering faxes to recipients in our office. There were five floors at Milberg Weiss, and all of them had individual employee offices, so I had to make my rounds to every floor delivering faxes maybe ten or more times a day. It definitely wasn't a job for someone who wasn't in shape, and I went through at least two pairs of running shoes while working in the fax room.

Working at the firm didn't make me feel as uncomfortable as one might think. Obviously all of the attorneys were educated, including many of the staff members, but I didn't feel incompetent. I definitely was conscious of the fact that no one in the office had likely experienced what I had or had experienced any semblance of my upbringing or background, but I didn't feel uncomfortable or out of place. I wasn't naïve either. I wasn't under any illusion that no one in the office judged me or looked down on me because who I was and where I had been. I was from a totally different walk of life than most of them and was a twenty-three-year-old black male from the hood who wasn't far removed from prison. I was also aware that my mannerism and speech may have at times been different than what was typical in that environment. I had actually become aware of the same thing while still in prison and socializing with Ben and others from the public speaking and sales training classes. I had an open mind, wanted to grow and get better, but I had no intention of changing things over which I had no control. I was comfortable in my own skin and Milberg Weiss's unique culture helped.

After working at Milberg for a period of time I started growing in almost every area of my life outside of work as well as within the firm. Most of my experiences at Milberg Weiss was wonderful and allowed me to grow, not only professionally but also socially. Those experiences helped catapult me to an educational and professional path that would have been unimaginable for me only a few years earlier. There's no question the firm was an alien world for me when I first started working there and was no easy adaption, but it was one of the best experiences of my life, and I wouldn't be where I am today without that place and people there.

The most influential person at the firm for me, without question, was Patrick. I hadn't had much communication with him initially. One day I was on one of my fax deliveries going floor to floor, and when I came to Patrick's office to drop off a fax, he asked me to close the door and have a seat.

I had been at the firm for only a few months, and all I had done was deliver the hell out of some faxes and stay out of the way. I knew that working at the law firm was a world far from where I had ever been, and my conduct was probably being closely watched because of how I got the job and where I had just come from some seven months prior.

I was scared shitless that the powerful attorney I had no idea even knew me would tell me to close his office door and have a seat. All kinds of thoughts were going through my mind in those few seconds as I closed the office door and proceeded toward Patrick's desk to take a seat at the chair facing him. Thoughts of what did I do continued to cross my mind. There were a lot of pretty women at the firm, but I never said anything to anyone in a disrespectful way, or at least I had hoped I didn't. The dress code was very casual, with some of the women dressing like they were going out to a night club and others dressing like they were headed to the beach. After being in prison for almost five years, maybe my eyes were a little too focused on the women. I honestly had no idea why I was sitting there.

Within a minute Patrick made me feel more at ease than any of the other attorneys, including the associates, since I had started working at the firm. Basically he introduced himself to me, but in a less formal way, and we sat and had a chat. We talked for a few minutes about how I thought things were going for me at the firm so far, and then we ventured a little bit into my past and my plans for the future.

For someone of Patrick's stature within the firm to take the time to single me out and introduce himself and then take the time to get to know me a little meant a lot to me. No other attorney in the firm had done that to this point and Patrick was a big-time partner in the firm. His friendliness was a confidence booster, considering who he was and his position in the firm and that he took the time out of his busy schedule not only to introduce himself to me but also to be genuinely interested in who I was as a person and not just the felon who was hired from some at-risk inner-city program.

In the business world I would have been considered by many to be at the bottom of the totem pole, and most business people would have treated me that way, especially considering my past. As much as I cherished the opportunity I was given to work at the firm, and I have a lot of great memories as a fax clerk, there were a few people who made me feel less than. Some of it was subtle and some of it was not so subtle, but whenever I communicated with Patrick, I never felt I was being judged because of who I was or who I used to be. No matter how busy he was, he always had an open-door policy with me. Patrick would become one of my biggest supporters in the firm.

I can sit here and write a thousand stories about how Patrick positively influenced my life, but then this whole book would be about him, so to sum it up briefly, let's just say that many of the successes I've had can be attributed in a big way to Patrick. He made me feel like I wasn't just an uneducated felon who worked in the fax room. He made me believe I could accomplish anything even if I couldn't, and I admit some of my goals were unrealistically lofty at the time. I started believing this ex-gang member, high-school dropout, and felon, could go anywhere in life without regard to my past. I owe a lot of that confidence to Patrick.

As my life continued to prosper I would always thank Bruce for telling me about Triple Crown and subsequently introducing me to Ray

Smith. That was the break I needed and had wanted badly, and Bruce led me right to it. If I had never met Ray Smith, I never would have met Mike Duckor or joined High Hopes, and I would not have gotten a job at Milberg Weiss, and I might not be where I am today. I know Bruce is looking down on me from heaven saying, "Damn! You came a long way, LB!"

After Bruce and I were released from the halfway house we remained good friends and continued our work with High Hopes. Bruce had also landed a job at a prominent law firm in downtown San Diego, and we occasionally met up for lunch and talked about how far we'd come, not only from our days in prison and then our most recent days at the halfway house, but even going back as far as our days in the late 1980s when we were quasi enemies.

Rest in peace, my brother Bruce.

CHAPTER **23**

Parent Time

MY LIFE DIDN'T suddenly become perfect after being released from prison and getting a job at the law firm. It actually felt like the opposite at times while facing daily struggles that most people face. However, my station in life was on a steady incline because of the decisions I was making. My number-one obligation was providing for my children and ensuring that they lived in a safe and comfortable environment. I was determined to make sure that my children would never have any excuses not to become successful. If my children didn't realize their dreams it would not be because they grew up poor, without a father, and with limited opportunities. My salary working in the fax room wasn't much but it was a few dollars above minimum wage and it gave me the opportunity to provide for my family.

My daughter Selina was my oldest. I didn't have much of a relationship with her prior to going to prison. Unlike my relationship with Lamontt Jr.'s mother, Selina's mother and I were never in a relationship. Selina had been born when I was still in high school and I only saw her sparingly before I went to prison. However, I remember my experience growing up without a father and knowing the importance of having both parents in your life, so I wanted to step up now and do what was right.

Once I was released from prison Selina and Lamontt Jr. became my number-one priority. I eventually developed a strong relationship with Selina's grandmother Rose who had been caring for her most of her life while Selina's mother and I were trying to grow up and while I was in prison.

Unlike my situation with Selina, Lamontt Jr., who was five years old when I was released from prison, already had a relationship with me. He was only a month old when I was arrested, but I had been in a serious relationship with Cynthia. She would bring Lamontt Jr. to visit me often during my eight-month stay in MCC, and continued to visit after I was moved to prisons in Arizona and Texas. Cynthia and I would eventually grow apart and no longer have a girlfriend-boyfriend relationship, however she continued to write me letters to keep me updated on Lamontt Jr.'s progress and activities and send me pictures of him throughout my time in prison.

While I was in prison I cultivated a relationship with Lamontt Jr. It was extremely important to me, though, because I knew as a black male he needed me to step up and be a strong positive role model for him. I had no doubts that Cynthia was a good mother and would take care of my son the best that she could, but I had to be there to help raise him and I wasn't going to leave anything to chance.

My ultimate goal was to have a close relationship with both Selina and Lamontt Jr. I wanted to be an active participant in their daily lives, whether I got along well with either of their mothers or even if they lived in a different city or state. I suffered immensely from my parents' nonexistent co-parenting after their divorce. I was determined to not allow any baby mama drama prevent me from being the constant in my children's life. I was determined to be the best father I could and ensure my children would not have a childhood like my own.

No matter how hard I was working at the firm, how involved I was with High Hopes, how much work I did in the community, or how rigorously I worked getting through classes at the community college, striving to be a great father had always been paramount to what I perceived to be successful. My ambition and desire to succeed professionally and financially were important, but nothing meant more to me than being there for my children. Besides dedicating a great deal of my time to my children, working eight hours a day at least five days a week at the firm, and doing everything else in between, I did manage to squeeze in somewhat of a social life.

I had dated on and off since I was in the halfway house and had been in a couple of serious relationships. I had lived a very fast life and was knocking on thirty years old. I met Ellen at a beach party. The first time we met I told her she was going to be my wife. Of course I was just joking when I said it, but after three up and down years of dating, we finally tied the knot.

When Ellen and I got married we ended up blending our families. She already had two kids when we met, her daughter Ashlea, who was six years old, and her daughter Tiffani, who was three. Selina would eventually move in with us when she was thirteen and Lamontt Jr. would follow when he turned fifteen. It would be five years after we were married before Ellen and I got pregnant and brought our daughter Zaria into the world.

Seven years removed from prison and I was doing everything I had promised myself I would do in regard to my children and myself, even though professional success and financial stability would come at a snail's pace. I had an average income coupled with Ellen's salary, and we gradually put ourselves in a position to afford a middle-class lifestyle. I made a commitment that my children, including my step-daughters, would not experience living in a neighborhood inundated with gang and illegal drug activity. See what you did Ben by telling me I was a winner and having me actually believe it?

CHAPTER 24

I Think I Can Be a Lawyer

HAVING A SECOND chance was all that I had hoped for when I was in prison. My opportunity to be a father to my children was by far the best thing that came from my second chance. I was also finally able to contribute something positive to society instead of contributing to its destruction.

I was able to dream while in prison, but my second chance gave me the opportunity to realize my dreams. I was no longer the same person. I was no longer LB or Gunsmoke. I wasn't that guy anymore. I may have the label of felon, but that's not who I was. I was a former gang member. I was a former drug dealer. And I didn't have to allow it to control my future. I own my past.

My unwavering desire to pursue my dreams and ensure that my children never had to live the way I did as a child consumed my thoughts and affected me in ways I never thought were possible. I owed it to myself. I owed it to my children. I owed it to my mother.

I knew that I would need to work harder and continue pursuing my education to ensure I had the tools to even realistically dream about having an opportunity to fully realize my dreams. However, I don't think anything could have prepared me for the intellectual, emotional, psychological, spiritual, professional, and financial challenges I was about to face. I hadn't arrived yet, and I was about to find out how difficult it would be to get there.

School had never come easy for me, and neither did I embrace the academic environment while growing up. I didn't think about it much back then, but in hindsight I know exactly what the problem was for my academic failures. I had too much going on in my personal life at home and in my community to focus on school. On those few days I did attend school, I either ditched class or gravitated toward the things and people I thought I had something in common with, which usually involved hanging out with gang members and smoking weed and drinking alcohol between classes.

I accept some responsibility for my own actions that contributed to my dismal academic years, particularly when I got to junior high and high school. Regardless of how I grew up and turned out as a teenager and young adult, there was a time as a young kid that I actually thought about becoming a lawyer.

I remember watching *Perry Mason* on television with my mother and dreaming about what it would be like to become a lawyer. Perry Mason was a fictional character that gave me a temporary escape from my environment and gave me hope of a better life someday. It was interesting to watch how brilliant Attorney Perry Mason was and how he won every case. I wouldn't learn until I became an adult that it didn't matter how talented the attorney rarely has any lawyer won every one of his or her cases.

I also watched *Matlock* another one of my mother's favorites. Matlock was a lawyer similar to Perry Mason, and he too was clever and won every case. My mother would sit and watch reruns of *Matlock* for hours. I sat with her and watched it too on many occasions. I think this early experience may have planted a seed in me that would influence decisions I later made on my path to becoming a lawyer. Maybe my mother was on to something that I was not aware of.

It wasn't until I met a lawyer while at Lompoc who had also been a regular student in Ben's public speaking class that I once again started thinking of a possible career in the legal field. I wasn't sure I was college material and definitely wasn't convinced I had the ability to succeed in law school. While only thinking about it in passing, I knew even back then that if I ever chose the path to become a lawyer I would face insurmountable obstacles.

Shortly after being released from the halfway house I began taking classes at the local community college. I took a class or two here and there, but nothing too challenging. Once I started working at the law firm, becoming a lawyer no longer seemed unrealistic. Within months of working at the firm my focus on someday attending law school became a priority. Working in an environment with so many talented and successful lawyers motivated me from the outset to push myself to my capable limits.

I was fortunate early on in my rehabilitation to understand how important an education could be as a vehicle for overcoming my past. Even though I never liked school or was very good at it, I knew I didn't have to be the smartest person to become successful. As Ben would say, "It's not about being the smartest person; it's about being smart enough to realize you need to surround yourself with people who are smarter than you." I didn't take all of Ben's advice, but this piece of advice was something I held onto while I was still at the camp and once I was released from prison.

I had barely survived three and a half years of high school before dropping out. I had an above average IQ, but law school? Becoming a lawyer? Someone like me with all of the baggage I had and lack of excellent academic preparation? For some this would have been a pipe dream. However, it became a dream that I realistically believed could come true.

Don't get me wrong; I was still keenly aware of the many barriers that were in front of me, particularly my lack of academic preparation and my felony convictions; however, I made the decision not to allow any barriers curtail my hope and desire of being accepted to law school. I had to get the best college education I could and earn my college degree. As far as the felonies on my record, I would cross that bridge once I got there, but in the interim I researched how other felons got accepted to law school and became attorneys. Earning good grades in challenging courses more than occasionally, researching and discovering how a lot of attorneys had overcome felony convictions, some even more serious than mine, gave me a reason to believe in myself even more.

After taking my first batch of college courses at the community college, I knew that I was nowhere near being academically prepared for a four-year university. I started off by taking mostly general education classes.

As I got more comfortable with attending college and my academic confidence grew, I started carrying a heavier load of classes each semester. During some of my most intense semesters I had a full schedule, enrolled in one or two classes in the morning prior to going to work, worked eight hours, had another one or two classes in the evening after work, and then had a Saturday morning or afternoon class.

As time went by I continued my academic pursuit. Along with work, school, being involved in the community, and my family obligations, I had also become active in my church. The thought of becoming a minister had occasionally seeped into my brain. I was focused on being able to contribute my best to my church, and seminary school, not law school, became more prevalent in my immediate plans.

DON'T LET YOUR PAST HOLD YOU BACK

Generally it takes four to six years for a student to earn a "four-year college degree," it took me eleven years of going to school at night and on the weekends while also working full time and raising a family. After I graduated from college I made plans to prepare for the law school admission test, the LSAT, but as they say, "the spirit had been nudging on my heart," and before I had a chance to apply to law school, I applied and got accepted to seminary school in a master's of divinity program.

But I still had a strong desire to continue a career in law. After spending a full day in new-student orientation, I never returned to seminary school and was back on my mission to get accepted to law school.

There's a huge difference between dreaming of going to law school and actually getting into law school. I had been working in the legal field for a number of years before I started making serious preparations to go to law school. I heard the horror stories about not only the difficulties of law school itself once you're there but also how difficult it was to get accepted. I knew that if it was difficult for some of the very bright people who in many cases had come from affluent backgrounds, it would be a daunting task for someone like me.

The application process for getting accepted to law school can be intimidating to say the least. It can consume a prospective law student. Working on several drafts of a personal statement or essay, preparing for and taking the LSAT, and then preparing to send all of your law school applications to the various schools you applied to, can take almost a year or longer.

The legal market has become inundated with lawyers in almost every state, and one way to regulate the industry and control the number of new lawyers is to make getting into law school and particularly to pass the bar exam more difficult. I knew this fact going in to the application process, and considering my less-than-stellar academic preparation and my prison background, my chances of getting accepted to law school were slim, but my philosophy since prison was, "What did I have to lose?" I was all about turning my life around and being upwardly mobile, and if law school was a way to help me get there, I was going to go for it no matter the difficulty or odds against me.

After spending over a year preparing to send off my law school applications, studying for and taking the LSAT, and doing a lot of praying in between, I finally applied to law school. Even with my knowledge of the fierce competition for earning a spot in law school, and my less than stellar academic background and LSAT score, I was more concerned about my criminal past being the biggest obstacle for getting accepted.

I knew my chances of getting an acceptance letter to law school was a very long shot. I still had some hope because I put in the work; in fact I worked harder than I ever had. However, as each denial letter came in, my spirit got more crushed. Being rejected by so many law schools after I worked so hard was a major hit to my confidence. I wondered how many of the schools actually seriously considered accepting me. I was not prepared for such an overwhelming rejection.

When it was all over, I got rejected by every single law school I applied to. I suspected after seeing my LSAT score and learning I was a felon, one law school didn't even bother to finish reviewing my application. This school responded with a rejection letter within a few weeks of my application being submitted, which is lightning speed in the law school application world. And the rejection letter addressed me as *Ms. Bowens* instead of Mr. Bowens. To add insult to injury, the letter stated that I wasn't the kind of student they accepted, whatever that meant. I could have allowed all of the rejection letters kill my spirit, but at least a couple of the schools in their rejection letter included a personal note telling me that I needed to become more competitive and don't give up.

DON'T LET YOUR PAST HOLD YOU BACK

Perseverance had become one of my greatest assets but also one of my most difficult, because I became borderline hardheaded. I don't know why walking away from my pursuit of a law degree would be so difficult for me to accept. I still had my job at the firm. My family was being supported. I had already beaten most odds by not returning to prison, by earning my college degree, and by raising my family and maintaining my good citizenship within my community. I was a winner for all intents and purposes, and was doing reasonably well.

Prior to preparing for my second attempt at getting accepted to law school, I had to do some intense soul searching. I had to determine if this was a fight I was willing to take on once again. It had been time consuming and such a grueling ordeal the first time around that I needed to convince myself I was ready to do it all over again. I came to the decision relatively quickly that it was worth it, and this time I would enroll in an LSAT prep class.

Ellen and I were doing okay financially, but we were far from doing well. We had five kids between us, a mortgage, and other financial obligations. I knew my LSAT score was one of the main reasons I wasn't competitive the first time I applied to law school, so if I was going to give myself a better chance, this time around I would need to significantly increase my LSAT score. Ellen told me that she would continue to support my goal of attending law school, and we agreed that we would use a credit card to pay for the $1,300 LSAT prep class.

The LSAT prep classes were held four times a week—three nights a week and on Saturday morning. I kept prep materials with me at all times so I could study whenever I had a chance, including at work and in the bathroom. I would sometimes get up in the middle of the night for a bathroom run and study. I dedicated every available moment I had to studying for the LSAT and working on my applications. I also knew my LSAT score alone would not be high enough to offset other deficiencies in my application, so I enrolled in an MBA program to increase my competitiveness. There was nothing I could do about my criminal history except explain it to the best of my ability, but I had control over my LSAT and future academic performance. I had heard somewhere that you should worry about only the things you have control over, and that's what I was doing. The rest would have to take care of itself.

My confidence started growing after every LSAT prep class and practice test. I still knew I had a long way to go before my score would be competitive, and standardized testing was not an area I was strong in, but the little tricks the class taught me and consistent practice helped prepare me to increase my score. Unfortunately law schools did not take the highest LSAT score out of an applicant's multiple scores but instead averaged the scores, so even if I scored higher on my second try it would have to be high enough to make an impactful difference.

By the time it came around for me to retake the LSAT I had prepared myself adequately to give it my best shot with the mental capabilities and test taking skills I had. After I took the test a second time, it took a few weeks for me to receive my score. When I finally got my score back I was happy. I wasn't going to Harvard Law School or any other law school in its ranking vicinity, but my LSAT score had increased and I was definitely a more competitive applicant.

My hard work and perseverance had paid off. I also reworked my personal statement. I thought I had a compelling story, but I needed to show that I also had the ability for academic success. I was aware of the fact that no matter how compelling my story was and what I'd overcome, if the law schools didn't believe I could succeed academically, I probably had no shot at getting in.

What I emphasized in my personal statement was my unrelenting desire to succeed and persevere. Instead of trying to minimize or run from my past, this time around I owned my personal statement and tried to convey that I was exactly the kind of student the school wanted.

After a lot of hard work and prayer, I applied to law school once again. Unlike the first time when I applied, the second time I only applied to seven schools instead of ten. I also applied only to schools I thought I had a realistic chance of getting into. After about three weeks of submitting all of my applications, I would take a lunch break every day, leave work, and drive all the way from downtown San Diego to my home in East Chula Vista, which was about fourteen miles each way. I was so anxious that I wanted to time my lunch breaks with the time our mail was delivered, so I could see if I received any letters from law schools.

I knew that the larger the envelope the more likely it was an acceptance letter, because the law schools enclosed material relevant to the matriculation process. All my previous letters from law schools had been thin with a one-page letter enclosed, often with boilerplate language beginning with, "We regret to inform you" or "Unfortunately." However, this time around I was not looking for a skinny letter or the words *regret* or *unfortunately*. My brain was set on the larger thick envelope with the first word on the letter inside being *Congratulations*.

I remember leaving work and going home for lunch like I had done for probably a couple of months and pulling up to my mailbox. Each time I had opened the mailbox, the first thing and likely the only thing I would be looking for was mail from a law school. On this day, after already receiving two rejections, I opened the mailbox to a huge envelope from a law school. My first law-school acceptance came from North Carolina Central a historically black college.* It was a surreal moment for me. I got my first acceptance into law school. Regardless of my prior law-school admission rejections, I finally had the opportunity to realize my dream of attending law school.

After receiving that first acceptance letter, from that point on it didn't really matter if I got denied by the remaining schools. I knew coming that fall I would be matriculating as a law student. All my hard work and perseverance had paid off and had been conveyed in that one acceptance letter. When all the law schools had responded to my applications for admission, I would get accepted to three of the seven schools, including Golden Gate University in San Francisco, one of the law schools that initially denied me but gave me the advice that I needed to become more competitive. I decided that my best option was to go to law school in San Francisco because it would be close enough for me to jump on a quick Southwest flight home, but far enough away that I could focus and not flunk out.

CHAPTER 25

Law School Daze

BACK IN MAY of 1993 I had made the trip from Lompoc Federal Prison to a halfway house in San Diego. Now in August of 2007 I was making a trip from San Diego to San Francisco to attend law school. Had I finally overcome my past? At least that's what I thought for a few weeks leading up to my first day of law school.

A funny thing about the law school experience, and I'm sure most attorneys would attest to: it doesn't matter how smart you are or think you are law school has a way of making you humble. For some people it's the first time they aren't the smartest person in their class. After all of the excitement I had leading up to matriculation it didn't take long to question whether I might be in over my head.

On the first day of orientation I was required to go to the school bookstore and purchase all my textbooks for the semester. I was in the evening program so I could work full-time and had only four classes during my first semester, but when I got to the bookstore and gave the clerk the list of classes and required texts, I almost had a heart attack. I spent almost a thousand dollars for textbooks for only four classes. Each textbook was at least an inch and a half thick, and once I had a chance to sit down and read the syllabi for my classes and reading list, I realized that I would be reading almost every page of my textbooks. If I had any arrogance or cockiness after finding out I got into law school, it dissipated that first day of orientation.

There's no argument that many folks with my past do not end up in law school. I knew this truth going in and thought I would be prepared for whatever law school had to throw at me. I had anticipated the academics to be the most challenging part of law school for me, but it was the culture. I was culture shocked. I started off in the evening program with older students, or at least students who worked and may have had families and had some life experience like me. Most students sitting next to me were recent college graduates, and some were ten or fifteen years younger than me. I already knew and could tell by the way some of them acted that many of them had come from very affluent backgrounds and were probably some of the best and brightest. To say I was little intimidated would be an understatement.

My first class was contracts. The professor went around the room and had all the students introduce themselves and give a brief bio. Being shy around people I don't know and already feeling a little intimidated about the academic rigor and cultural challenges I was facing, I was a little nervous to introduce myself. I had already heard at least a dozen or so students introduce themselves and list their academic accomplishments. Most of them went to top colleges and universities, and some of them had graduate degrees from prestigious programs. As I listened to each student I thought, *Wow, I'm in a class with a bunch of overachievers.*

I may not have been able to compete with them academically, I had something most of those kids didn't, and that was an unrelenting will to succeed against all odds, and that even meant law school. I had already endured so much throughout my life that law school was the last thing I was going to allow to break me. So when my contracts professor called on me to give a brief introduction of myself, I held my head high, my chest out, and introduced myself, and from that day on I put my head down and worked my tail off to stay there.

Although I worked harder than I ever had before while I was in law school, close to the end of my first semester of law school and after midterms I was in serious academic trouble. I was studying as much as I possibly could when I wasn't working, but to no avail. The dean of Student Services called me into her office and informed me that I had been placed on academic probation, and if I didn't bring my grades up by the end of the year I would be academically disqualified from law school.

One thing about law school, and I'm sure it's probably the same for other professional programs such as medical school, dental school, etc., is that there is no coddling of students. You are in big boy and big girl school, so you either step up and make the cut or step out and be academically disqualified. The only thing that was somewhat comforting to me about my dire academic situation was that many of my fellow classmates, who I thought were better prepared academically, were also in the same boat. It was kind of funny to me because a lot of them wouldn't even talk to me as if I was below them. Of course I wasn't hoping for anyone's failure, even in the fiercely competitive environment of law school, but it actually made me laugh because many of the students who were struggling academically like I was were the same students who were snooty toward me. And here we all were about to flunk out of law school together. Through this challenging period, I was still determined to get it together academically and succeed. Success was the only option; I just had to dig deep and figure out how to succeed.

Ellen and I had starting having serious marital problems during my first semester, so the news of academic probation and likely disqualification couldn't have come at a worse time, and it would soon get even worse. When I came home to San Diego for the winter break after my first semester of law school, my marriage started falling apart. We had been having problems even before I left for law school, but upon my return and after a heated argument, my marriage was over, and I was headed for a divorce during my first year of law school while facing academic disqualification.

After returning to law school for the spring semester, I was separated from Ellen and missing my two-year-old daughter Zaria terribly. My spirits were not high, to say the least. I was in danger of losing not only my family but also my dream of earning my law degree and someday becoming a lawyer. At the time I had a lot of animosity toward Ellen because I wanted to try to work on our relationship and save my family, but as time went on I stopped blaming her for the demise of our marriage. I realized that marriage takes a lot of work and is hard, and people fall out of love. I didn't have a lot of mental energy to expend on my sorrows over getting a divorce. My energy had to be used to survive my first year of law school, and any emotional or mental anguish over losing my family would have to wait until the summer. I had to excel academically in my second semester.

Still dealing with the cultural shock of law school, rigorous academic requirements, immense financial burdens, the possibility of flunking out, and the inevitability of a divorce, I was miserable during my second semester of my first year in law school. Although I had some enjoyable times hanging out with my core cohort, those times were overshadowed by the stress. Failure was not an option. Adding to my pressure to succeed in my first year of law school, I did not want to get disqualified. I had already secured a position with my firm as a summer associate, which made it even more imperative that I raise my grades and survive the first year. As a summer associate I would be compensated like an attorney for the summer and have an opportunity to work on challenging projects as though I were an attorney. A summer associate was a coveted position for law students, usually the summer after their second year in law school, and reserved for students coming from the top law schools and who had the highest grades. Neither of those requirements had applied to me, but the firm believed in me enough to give me an opportunity, so the thought of having to inform the firm that I couldn't accept the summer associate position because I was disqualified from law school seemed daunting. I was going to do everything within my power to not make that a reality.

One of the first things I did right before the start of my second semester of law school was that I took out an extra amount of money in student loans for living expenses, so I could take a leave from work for the semester and focus solely on school. After I secured enough financing to pay my bills and still contribute to the support of my family back home without working during the semester, I put all my effort in doing well in school. I put my head down, worked hard, put the rest in God's hands, and didn't come up for air until my last final exam and the semester was over.

After I finished all my final exams, I got on a plane and went back to San Diego for the summer. I knew it was going to take a few weeks before all my professors posted their grades online and I would know whether I made the cut and was still a law student. I knew I didn't need all A's or B's to prevent disqualification, but I needed to do well. All I really needed was at least one A along with a couple of solid B's, and I would be out of the woods. I even had room for a high C or two. My life was in the balance for those few weeks of waiting for my grades to be posted. Everything I had worked so hard for was on the line. I had to put the summer associate position on hold until I got my grades, because there was no way I would start with the risk of being fired because I was no longer in law school. I checked online almost every hour of every day to see if my grades were posted. The grades were posted on a rolling basis, as each professor graded his or her final exams. Waiting for my professors to post their grades felt like I was waiting for my doctor to tell me whether I had a terminal disease.

I know grades cannot even come close to the gravity of a terminal illness, but after working so hard for something and possibly having it taking away from me because of an arbitrary grade point average was a terrible feeling.

Finally in late May my grades started coming in online. A couple of the first grades posted were B's. I wasn't out of the woods yet. I needed all my grades to be posted before I would know for certain that I wasn't disqualified, and a low C or a D would significantly lower my grade point average and likely be the end of my short-lived law school career. When that last grade posted a little over two weeks after the first one, I made the cut! I didn't flunk out. Not only did I make the cut and survive my first year of law school, but I also received an academic honor by earning the Cali Award for Excellence, which meant I had the second highest grade in my class.

Although I had been knocked down to earth after initially believing I had arrived when I got accepted to law school, those challenges during my first year of law school and coming out a winner helped me get some of my confidence back. Even some of my classmates who were snooty towards me during my first year suddenly started kissing my ass and asking me if I wanted to join one of their study groups. What a difference surviving the first year of law school and winning a Cali award made.

Although I had survived the first year of law school, I would never become an academic superstar or fully enjoy the experience. Succeeding in my first year definitely gave me the confidence I needed to compete and finish law school, but going through a divorce, missing my family, working, taking a full load of classes every semester including during the summer semesters, and having financial problems, all made my final years of law school less than enjoyable. It had become just a means to an end. I now knew how to study and pass my classes and that's all that mattered to me.

215

DON'T LET YOUR PAST HOLD YOU BACK

After my first year in law school, I wanted to finish law school as soon as possible so I could retake control of my life and close that chapter. Law school had become a miserable experience despite the occasional parties and get-togethers with my friends from my section with whom I had become close to. My active participation in various student organizations, including being the vice president of the Black Law Students Association (BLSA) also made life in law school a little more bearable. But overall, law school sucked.

After all the highs and lows, the painstaking sacrifices, the perseverance through it all against enormous odds, in December 2010, I finally graduated from law school. My earning my law degree had less to do with me actually having a strong desire to become a lawyer and more to do with me wanting to prove to myself and everyone else I could overcome my past and succeed. Not only did I get accepted to law school, but I also succeeded there and graduated a semester early. An average, mediocre student who was a high school dropout, former gang member, and felon had earned a law degree from a fully accredited law school.

My story could have ended at earning my law degree. I had already overcome my own personal Mount Everest. Under most people's standards I had nothing else to prove. I had much to be proud of, and I was proud. I had succeeded against the odds. I even defied the odds. What was strange, however, even considering the hell I had gone through to get into law school and then survive it, was that I now had an unquenchable desire to reach even higher.

CHAPTER **26**

Raising the Bar

MY PRISON AND law school experiences would be walks in the park compared to conquering the bar exam and becoming a licensed attorney. I had already gone through one of the most difficult stretches of my life and achieved beyond my expectation. Why would I continue to put myself through purgatory just to pass an exam? No matter what I accomplished, this chapter of my life would not be complete until I passed the bar exam and became a licensed attorney.

For years I had heard all of the horror stories about the bar exam, particularly while I worked for the firm and during law school. However, little did I know that I was about to go on a journey that would be far more challenging emotionally, mentally, physically, and spiritually than my upbringing in the inner city, my time in prison, and my law-school experiences combined. If surviving law school had shown me what I was made of, conquering the bar exam would prove my destiny.

I was a law school graduate, and the only thing left was passing the bar exam and going full speed ahead with my career objectives. I knew that tons of people had law degrees and weren't licensed and were very successful, and I knew this could be the path for me, because I had plans outside of practicing law even if I never stepped foot in a courtroom.

In addition to the bar exam, I had to be successful on my moral character application. Even if I passed the bar I wouldn't be able to practice law until my moral character application was approved. All applicants had to submit this application to the State Bar for a thorough background check to determine if applicants had good moral standing and could be trusted to represent the bar appropriately. Because of my serious criminal background, the moral character application process would be like passing the bar exam.

Most applicants for admission to practice law have their moral character applications approved within three months because there usually isn't any serious issue with their past. However, that would be a different story for me. Even though I had graduated from law school and had not been involved in any criminal activity since being arrested in January 1989, almost two decades earlier, trying to get my moral character cleared so I could practice law would take me on another relentless and grueling journey.

At the very beginning of the moral-character process I was asked to submit any and all official documentation of my criminal past, credit history, employment history since I was eighteen, and residential history for the previous ten years. After obtaining all these documents I had to send them to the bar committee for review. As soon as I thought I had submitted everything that the committee needed, it would request more documentation, and I had to repeat the process once again. As I waited to have my moral character application approved, I rigorously prepared to take the bar exam at least twice.

After a year and a half of preparing and sending documentation to the bar committee regarding my moral character application, the committee informed me that it had all of the documentation it needed to make a decision but I would need to first sit for an informal hearing. It was basically my last chance to convince the committee that I had good moral character to be an attorney. Just like when I was going through my personal, academic, and financial challenges during law school, I felt like there was some power behind closed doors trying to prevent me from realizing my dream of becoming an attorney.

I asked John, one of my mentors and confidants at the firm, to attend the hearing with me. I trusted John's counsel and needed his moral support. John wouldn't be allowed to speak on my behalf at the hearing, but in case the committee subsequently denied me, I could appeal their decision and have legal counsel represent me.

There were four committee members at the moral-character hearing, and we were sitting at a long square table. John and I were sitting next to each other at the top of the table, and one committee member sat on each side of us while two sat directly in front of the end of the other side of the table and me. I was asked a barrage of questions about my criminal history, my finances, and many other things, but the topic I thought might prevent me from having my moral character approved was the 1988 Christmas night incident when a rival gang member was murdered. I was right. I was grilled on what happened on Christmas night. At one time during the hearing one of the committee members who was the only male, asked me if I had any remorse for what happened. I explained to the committee the situation that night and how I was remorseful about what happened. But I was not the shooter, nor did I instigate the situation. The committee had already read all of the police reports related to the shooting, including the affidavit for the search warrant, so they knew all of the details, but the committee members wanted to hear it from me, and I was completely candid.

As I discussed the Christmas night situation as well as my life in general and how I was trying to overcome my past and rehabilitate myself, I felt horrible. This was the first time I had been in front of a group of people to whom I had to prove I was worthy of something since Lompoc Prison, when I had to convince my case manager and counselor that I had deserved a halfway house.

219

DON'T LET YOUR PAST HOLD YOU BACK

I left that hearing feeling like crap. I remember telling John as we were driving back to the office that I didn't think I closed the deal. He said he thought I did a good job, but the way the committee grilled me, particularly the guy who asked me to explain myself about what happened on Christmas night 1988, I just knew there was no way they would clear my moral character regardless of what I had overcome and accomplished over the years.

About a month or so after my hearing with the bar committee, I was informed in a letter that my moral character application had been approved. It had been almost two years since I filed my application for moral character clearance. Now all I needed to do was pass the bar and I would be a licensed attorney. Passing the bar exam, however, would prove to be a monumental challenge in itself.

After my second year in law school, I wanted to graduate early because of all the personal challenges I had, so I took an overload of classes during the fall and spring semesters, in addition to taking a full load of classes during the summer. My grades suffered, which also prevented me from being adequately prepared for the bar exam. I knew that the bar exam would require all my attention and I started preparing early.

The first time I took the bar exam I didn't even come close to passing, but I knew I couldn't give up, so after getting the notice from the bar that I failed, I took a moment to thank God for my blessings, and I put my head back down and got back to studying. I was able to take a couple months off from work and take out a bar loan during my first attempt at the bar, but on my second attempt I couldn't afford to take much time off from work or get another bar loan. Therefore, I studied at night and on weekends for the bar exam my second time.

After I got my results back for my second bar exam, my score was higher, but once again I failed. I was also getting deeper in debt because of the expense of the bar exam, student loan debt, and living expenses. I couldn't get a high-paying job because not only was the economy still trying to recover from the Great Recession, but also I was not a licensed attorney and was eligible to be only a law clerk or paralegal.

I don't know if it was me being stubborn, dedicated, or both, but I knew I was going to have to pursue the bar exam once again. Prior to my third attempt at the bar exam, I began drinking alcohol more often and wasn't just a social drinker anymore. The stress of life and getting so close to a major accomplishment only to have it elude me was becoming too much, and I drank alcohol to deal with the emotional pain. However, I found a way to push myself and persevere through the bar exam for a third time.

On my third try I missed passing the bar exam by twenty points. This was the closest I had come, even though I was working fulltime, and it could have easily gone the other way for me. Twenty points was the equivalent of missing a few multiple choice questions or having one low score on just one essay out of six. In fact, the essay I believe caused me to fail was scored passing during the first reading, and then the second grader scored it ten points lower which caused the lower overall bar score.

I was beyond crushed after all of my sacrifices, blood, sweat, and tears were to no avail. One thing I did do after I got over the initial devastation and shock of failing the bar a third time was pray and thank God as I had after my two previous bar-exam failures. Although my spirits got lower after each bar failure, I thought about my mother's advice that no matter what I was going through, always give God praise. I didn't particularly feel like thanking God or praising Him for anything, but I opened my heart and thanked Him for the opportunity. Considering my background I shouldn't have even been sitting for a bar exam.

DON'T LET YOUR PAST HOLD YOU BACK

During some of the most difficult times in my life, especially dur-ing my five years in prison, I had never questioned God's existence. Through it all I maintained faith in God. That was until my repeated bar-exam failures. I had to accomplish this final feat to close that chapter in my life. I couldn't let it go until I was a licensed attorney. I had worked for it. I persevered. I had paid the price. I knew in my heart and mind I deserved it. My repeated failures at passing the bar exam would ultimately turn me away from God and more toward alcohol, which would deteriorate my emotional and physical health, causing depression, gallbladder disease, and pancreatitis.

If anyone had a reason to give up on becoming a licensed attorney it was me. I had earned a law degree, one of the most prestigious profes-sional degrees one could earn. I was just too stubborn to let the bar go and be content with how far I had come. I went back and forth as to whether I should put myself through the mental, emotional, spiritual, and financial burden of attempting to take the exam one more time. I could say it was perseverance, but at that point I was hardheaded and stubborn. I think God was trying to tell me, "Lamontt, let this bar exam go; you are killing yourself." But I couldn't let it go. Something inside kept telling me that failure wasn't an option.

Between my third and fourth attempts at passing the bar exam, I be-came a functioning alcoholic. I would drink excessively every day when I got home from work and then all day on the weekends. After my fourth attempt at the bar exam I pretty much had no more faith in the system. I compared the answers I wrote to the sample answers and it looked almost identical. I spotted most of the issues and felt like my analysis was close to the sample answers, but I still received a failing score.

Only a few people actually knew how difficult a time I was having over my bar exam failures. I didn't share my feelings much, and I was still taking care of business by going to work every day and paying my rent, though other creditors were being neglected. If it weren't for my law-school sweetheart Janee, who was in my corner and stood by me during this time more than anyone else, coupled with my love for Zaria, I may have given up. I remained in a spiritual funk during those years of studying for and failing the bar exam repeatedly, but I refused to give up on myself, and God didn't give up on me, even though I gave up on Him for a period of time.

I can call it perseverance or stubbornness, but I was not going to give up until I was a licensed attorney. I weathered my time in purgatory, attended Alcohol Anonymous, went to therapy, and eventually found my way back to God.

I decided to take a break from the bar and focus on work and getting my confidence back. During my break Zaria moved to Maryland with her mother, and I had been thinking about moving there. I knew that Maryland, particularly the DC/Baltimore area, offered more opportunities for African American professionals than California, particularly San Diego. And more importantly, I hadn't lived in the same city with Zaria since she was two years old. After coming so close to passing the California bar but coming up short by twenty points, I decided to take the Maryland bar instead. If becoming a lawyer was what I was determined to do, I had to be more strategic, and going outside of California was another option for me.

Every state has its bar exam on the same days as every other state, and it's given twice a year, once in July and once in February. I decided to take the bar exam the following year in February, and then I immediately began working on my moral character application for Maryland. I knew if it had taken me almost two years for California to approve my moral character to practice law, Maryland might take as long or longer. I also began studying in November. I had four months to prepare. I made the decision that it would be my final attempt at the bar exam, and if I couldn't pass in Maryland, then I was finally going to give up on my dream of being an attorney. I had already beaten astronomical odds in earning my law degree. I would just have to accept that achievement as the pinnacle of my legal accomplishment.

All bar exams are tough, with California being considered one of the toughest. But leading up to the Maryland bar I studied just as hard as I had for the California bar and maybe even harder, because I had to learn several subjects specifically related to Maryland law that I was totally unfamiliar with.

At the time of my Maryland bar prep I was living in Irvine, California, with my girlfriend and working in San Diego, which was about a two-hour Amtrak train ride each way. I used that time sitting on the train for four hours each day working and studying. I gave it all I had with studying for the Maryland bar exam. When February came around I flew to Maryland to sit for the bar exam.

Three months after I took the Maryland bar and on the day that my results were being released, I woke up that morning anxious and angry. I got up and got ready for work and went to the office as if it was a normal day, but I knew there was nothing normal about it. When I got to the office I closed my office door and wondered if I would have the courage to go online and see if I passed, once the pass-and-fail list was posted that afternoon at 1:00 pm.

My anticipation of the bar-exam results was beyond overwhelming. When 1:00 pm came I did not have the courage to go online to see whether I passed. I just looked at the clock and assumed that I had failed. It had occurred many times before that I assumed the bar gods disfavored me again.

As I allowed the time go beyond 1:00 pm without touching my computer, however, the strangest thing happened. At about 1:03 p.m. my girlfriend, Veronica, called my cell phone. She knew all about the bar exam results being released that day and my anxiety. All I could think was *why would she call me during a time like this when I was so depressed?* I assumed I had failed the bar exam once again. I didn't pick up the phone when she called. I just watched it go to voicemail. I couldn't talk about the bar at that time.

About two minutes went by after her first call and then Veronica called once again at 1:05 pm, and I still couldn't pick up. I said to myself once again, why is she calling me? Doesn't she know what I'm going through? I just failed the bar exam once again, and I don't feel like talking to anyone. Just let me sit in my office and languish in my misery.

Around 1:20 pm I decided to pick up my cell phone and listen to the voice message Veronica left. When I listened to her message it blew me out of this world. She had earlier insisted I give her my bar exam number, but I had no idea she would use it to check whether I passed. As I listened to the message it became as surreal as anything I had ever experienced. "Babe, you need to call me right away. I just checked your bar exam number, and you passed."

It was my first attempt at taking the Maryland bar exam, and I passed. To finally see my name on that bar exam pass list was one of the best feelings of my life. From that point it didn't matter if it took me multiple times to become a licensed attorney or I had to experience suffering to get there. I didn't care that most of my classmates had already been practicing law for years and were well ahead of me professionally. Once I passed the bar it didn't matter that I had spent at least ten thousand dollars or more on bar-exam-related expenses. When I passed the bar all that mattered was I was going to be a licensed attorney. I had enough faith in myself and in God again to persevere through all the disappointment and to be stubborn when I needed to be, to realize my dream.

I know some attorneys would never admit that they had such a difficult time becoming a licensed attorney. We attorneys are already somewhat arrogant and think we're smarter than everyone else. Who would admit such setbacks to a client or a potential employer? I'm sure some people who took the bar exam several times before they passed might never admit it. Once you pass you pass, no one has to know how many times it took you. Well in my case I guess everyone knows because I put it in my memoir. But you get my point.

Once I passed the bar and they approved my moral character, I was sworn in a month later and had finally become an attorney. My law school and bar-exam struggles taught me more about myself than any lesson I could have ever learned to that point, including my time in prison. Life could have been much easier for me, but I don't think I would have become the person that I am today. Like many other milestones in my life that I had to struggle, strive, and grind out to make a reality, becoming a licensed attorney was no different.

Back in 1989, being locked up for eight months in the Metropolitan Correctional Center was probably more difficult for me than it was growing up in the hood the twelve years prior. For the first time I was confined for an extended period of time without knowing how long it would last. I was a nineteen-year old gangbanger and ex-drug dealer in federal custody. I would spend most of my time staring for hours out of a really thick and narrow bulletproof window in a cell that was no bigger than most bathrooms in an average size home. I would look out over beautiful downtown San Diego and the bay, watching people walk by, hoping that one day I would get out of prison and make a better life for myself, my daughter, and my newborn son.

Fast forward to 2018, as I leave the law firm on my daily break for fresh air, I now walk past that same tall brown building where I was once confined for twenty-four hours a day, seven days a week, for eight long months. Now I look up at it from the outside, not as an inmate, but as an attorney. I can reflect on where I've been and where

I am today, and say, *"Look how far you've come, Lamontt. You are no longer LB aka Gunsmoke."*

Don't Let Your Past Hold You Back.

Being sworn in as an attorney

In the Judge's Chambers with my boss on the day of being sworn in

In the office on a beautiful Saturday

The day I was sworn in as an attorney

My homies 4 Life

Questions to Ponder

1. What does <u>Perseverance</u> mean to you?

2. What does <u>Forgiveness</u> mean to you?

3. What does <u>Change</u> mean to you?

Acknowledgments

I knew I wouldn't have a litany of people from the literary world to acknowledge once I decided to sit down, write this book myself, starting from scratch and then self-publish. However, I would be remiss if I didn't give a shout out to a number of special people. To my brother Rumell, thanks for your unrelenting pressure on me to become an attorney and finish this book. You didn't just talk you also backed it up with deeds. To the rest of my siblings: Annette, Rhonda, Darnell, Sonya, and Brandy. We got through this even with all the heartache and pain. To my dad, Big Rumell, aka Papa Smurf, thanks for stepping up the second time around. To my children: Selina, Lamontt Jr., Ashlea, Tiffani, and Zaria. Thanks for giving me a reason to turn my life around and persevere. Joy, Cynthia, and Ellen: thank you for my children. Dave aka Chippy, you are the quintessential example of a real day one homie. Ben Gay III, any success I've been blessed to experience since Lompoc, in some way, derives from you. Uncle Jesse you are the epitome of what family should be about. Thanks for being there for me during my first major test after prison. You saved me. Aunties Margret and Ann, I wish you were here to experience this with me. Mike Duckor and Ray Smith, thanks for the High Hopes! Bill Lerach and Kathi Strozza, thanks for taking a chance on me. Patrick Coughlin, I still don't understand why you believed in me—but you did—and I am forever grateful. Mike Dowd and John Grant, thanks a ton for the encouragement during this entire endeavor and giving me constructive criticism and feedback, even when it hurt my feelings.

Professor T. Ford, thank you for allowing me to pick your brain, reading drafts, and sharing your time and invaluable expertise. To all of my homies from the East Dago Mob '80s era, we know it was more than just a street gang. And to you, the reader, thanks for allowing me to share my story with you.

A Few Sources

Chapter 1
Gang. (n.d.). Retrieved from https://en.wikipedia.org/wiki/Gang

CA Penal Code § 186.22.a (2016). Retrieved from https://law.justia.com/codes/california/2016/code-pen/part-1/title-7/chapter-11/section-186.22.a/

The Cosby Show. Retrieved from https://en.wikipedia.org/wiki/The_Cosby_Show

Chapter 2
Crip Gangs in Los Angeles County | From Long Beach to Pomona (n.d.). Retrieved from http://www.streetgangs.com/crips#sthash.wCwuxQT4.dpbs

Blood gangs in Los Angeles (n.d.). Retrieved from http://www.street-gangs.com/bloods#sthash.m9klKmlw.dps

Chapter 3
Williams, A. (n.d.). The Full Story Of The 1980's Crack Epidemic Is Still Yet To Be Told. Retrieved from https://uproxx.com/hiphop/snowfall-1980s-crack-epidemic/4/

Chapter 5
Good, D. (Feb. 17, 2012). "It's a War Zone Down Here."
An exploration of the significantly high murder rates in Southeast
San Diego. Retrieved from http://www.sandiegomagazine.com/
San-Diego-Magazine/March-2012/Its-a-War-Zone-Down-Here/

Chapter 6
Dimon, L. (Dec. 3, 2013). Crip Walk: The Pop Culture Sensation
That Came From Violent Gangsters. https://mic.com/articles/75417/
crip-walk-the-pop-culture-sensation-that-came-from-violent-gang-
sters#.lX24oT53X
Gunsmoke. Retrieved from http://www.museum.tv/eotv/gunsmoke.
htm

Chapter 7
Ebert, R. (June 27, 2001). *Baby Boy*. Retrieved from https://www.
rogerebert.com/reviews/baby-boy-2001

Chapter 12
Rich, F.K. (2018). 40 Ounces of Fury! The Definitive Malt Liquor
Taste Test. Retrieved from
https://drunkard.com/03-03_forty_
fury/

Chapter 14
U. S. Indicts 22 on Narcotics, Weapons Charges. (1989, February
10). *Los Angeles Times*. Retrieved from http://articles.latimes.
com/1989-02-10/local/me
-2463_1_indictment-

The Drug Policy Alliance: A Brief History of the Drug War.
Retrieved from http://www.drugpolicy.org/issues/
brief-history-drug-war

Coates, T. (October 2015). The Black Family in the Age of Mass Incarceration. Retrieved from https://www.theatlantic.com/magazine/archive/2015/10/the-black-family-in-the-age-of-mass-incarceration/403246/

Chapter 15
Human Rights Watch. III. Incarceration and Race. Retrieved from https://www.hrw.org/reports/2000/usa/Rcedrg00-01.htm

Chapter 16
Chen, Michelle. (Aug. 17, 2015). Prison Education Reduces Recidivism by Over 40 Percent. Why Aren't We Funding More of It? Giving Prisoners Access to Financial Aid for College Tuition is the First Step Towards "De-carceration." Retrieved from https://www.thenation.com/article/prison-education-reduces-recidivism-by-over-40-percent-why-arent-we-funding-more-of-it/

Chapter 18
Markman, J., Durose, M., Rantala, R. & Tiedt, A. (June 2016). *Recidivism of Offenders Placed on Federal Community Supervision in 2005. Patterns from 2005 to 2010.* Retrieved from https://www.bjs.gov/content/pub/pdf/ropfcs05p0510.pdf

Prison Culture: How the PIC Structures Our World... A Prisoner's Words Describing The "Hole." (2011, July 18). Retrieved from http://www.usprisonculture.com/blog/2011/07/18/a-prisoners-words-describing-the-hole/

Chapter 24

Lovett, B. L. (2015). *America's Historically Black Colleges and Universities: A Narrative History, 1837-2009.* Macon, GA: Mercer University Press.

What the Author Is Up to Now

M. Lamontt Bowens lives in San Diego, California. In addition to being a fulltime parent, he works as a staff attorney at the law firm Robbins Geller Rudman & Dowd. When he is not preoccupied with being a parent or busy at the law office, his focus is on The Bowens Group, his nonprofit organization, as its President and Founder. If you wish to have him speak to your group, please visit thebowensgroup. net.

CPSIA information can be obtained
at www.ICGtesting.com
Printed in the USA
FSHW02n0946150618
49362FS